Michigan's Looking Glass River

by Kayak:

A Modern-Day Journey Down a Historic River

By Ted M. Reuschel

Chapbook Press

Chapbook Press

Schuler Books
2660 28th Street SE
Grand Rapids, MI 49512
(616) 942-7330
www.schulerbooks.com

ISBN 13: 9781943359936

Library of Congress Control Number: in file

Copyright © 2018, Ted Reuschel

All rights reserved.

No part of this book may be reproduced in any form without express permission of the copyright holder.

Printed in the United States by Chapbook Press.

CONTENTS

PREFACE
ACKNOWLEDGEMENTS
WATERSHED MAP
RIVER SECTION MAPS
✳ THE DREAM   1
✳ THE SOURCE: WHERE DOES THE RIVER REALLY BEGIN?   4
    UNDERSTANDING WATERSHEDS
✳ THE WHAT AND WHY OF COUNTY DRAINS   8
✳ NAVIGATING THE RIVER   13
    THE LEGAL ISSUE
    THE PHYSICAL ISSUE
✳ THE GHOST TOWN OF GLASS RIVER   17
✳ INTO THE MARSHLANDS   24
    THE ROLE OF THE FLOODPLAINS
✳ THE LAINGSBURG VICINITY   27
✳ "LIONS, TIGERS AND BEARS"   28
    THE WHITETAIL DEER
    THE BLACK BEAR
    COUGARS?
✳ ON THE RIVER – TRIP ONE
  (Upton to Babcock)   34
    THE BABCOCK LAKE AREA
✳ ON THE RIVER – TRIP TWO
  (Babcock to Old 27)   42
    CAMPING GROUNDS AND SETTLEMENTS
    LOWRY PLAINS
    THE REMY-CHANDLER INTERCOUNTY DRAIN

❋ ON THE RIVER – TRIP THREE
   (Old 27 to DeWitt)   **50**
      USE BY THE NATIVE AMERICANS
         Water Trails and Indian Green
         Foot Trails
         The Source of Essentials

❋ THE DEWITT VICINITY   **58**
      THE INTERURBAN CROSSING
      RIVER-PARKS AND MODERN ACCESS
      THE SETTLING OF DEWITT

❋ THE NAMINGS: DEWITT, CLINTON AND
   LOOKING GLASS   **64**
      DEWITT AND CLINTON
      LOOKING GLASS

❋ ON THE RIVER – TRIP FOUR
   (DeWitt to Airport)   **70**
      MCGUIRE PARK
      LAKE GENEVA
      IS IT SCHAVEY OR SCHOEWE?
      ABOUT THE WATER
         Water Levels
         Storm Water
         Clean Water Facilities
         Water Quality Tests
         With Many Thanks to the "Friends"
      THE NILES AND GROGER EXPERIENCE
      ABOUT BRIDGES

❋ ON THE RIVER – TRIP FIVE
   (Airport to Wacousta)   **82**
      AIRPORT ROAD BRIDGE
      LOWELL ROAD BRIDGE
      FRANCIS ROAD BRIDGE
      HERBISON ROAD BRIDGE # 1
      HERBISON ROAD BRIDGE # 2

❋ THE WACOUSTA VICINITY   **89**
      QUESTION # 1
         Past Testimony

　　　　Present Clues
　　　　Conclusion
　　QUESTION # 2
　　　　Past Testimony
　　　　Present Clues
　　　　Conclusion
　　QUESTION # 3
　　　　Past Testimony
　　　　Present Clues
　　　　Conclusion

※ON THE RIVER – TRIP SIX

　(Wacousta to Hinman)　　　　　　　　**96**
　　WACOUSTA ROAD BRIDGE
　　HARLOW'S LIVERY – THE ONE AND ONLY
　　BAUER AND WRIGHT ROAD BRIDGES
　　THE NILES SETTLEMENT
　　WILDERNESS LIFE
　　CONTINUING DOWNSTREAM

※ON THE RIVER – TRIP SEVEN

　(Hinman to Howe)　　　　　　　　　**105**
　　THE EAGLE CANAL

※ON THE RIVER – TRIP EIGHT

　(Howe to Cutler)　　　　　　　　　　**109**
　　SOME SPECIAL TREES
　　　　The Sycamores – Blotchy Giants
　　　　The Tamaracks – A Most Unusual Conifer
　　　　Adding Color
　　MONROE ROAD BRIDGE
　　CUTLER ROAD TIMBER BRIDGE

※ON THE RIVER – TRIP NINE

　(Cutler to Portland)　　　　　　　　**114**

※THE PORTLAND VICINITY　　　　　**119**

※REFLECTING　　　　　　　　　　　**124**

BIBLIOGRAPHY

INDEX

PREFACE

I like adventure. I like history. I like kayaking. And I like sharing my experiences in writing. What a treat it is when I can do all of these together. Such was the case with this account of my journey by kayak down the Looking Glass River. Just a few miles from the state capitol at Lansing, the Looking Glass runs for 70 miles from its source in Livingston County to its juncture with the Grand River at Portland. Yet it is an easily-overlooked gem, its relatively undeveloped wildness a pleasant surprise, especially being so near the nearly half million people who make up the Lansing-East Lansing Metropolitan Statistical Area.

Only a couple of centuries ago, of course, it was pure wilderness – save for the limited impact placed upon it by the Native Americans. Thereafter, the Looking Glass corridor slowly but steadily changed. The historic account of those changes is an intriguing one. While much of it is unique to the Looking Glass, many aspects are also applicable to other early explorations and uses along the other rivers of Michigan, and of other States as well.

We will review numerous accounts, ranging from early Native American dependence, to the travel and trials by the first pioneers on the river and within its corridor. We will examine the use of the river to power many saw and grist mills, the origin of early settlements and eventual communities, and the many growing pains which accompanied such changes. And as we do so, we will also experience the adventure of floating upon and re-discovering this timeless river.

Come along, and enjoy the journey.

Ted M. Reuschel

Notes:
As part of an effort to retain the flavor of this adventure, I have elected not to drastically separate it into chapters, but rather to make the narrative more continuous, just as the river itself flows uninterrupted from one end to the other. Instead, major subject and day-trip changes will be noted simply by special larger type, surrounded by these icons:

※ LIKE THIS ※

The narrative will frequently move back and forth between river journey descriptions and historical accounts that relate to the particular location. To aid the reader in distinguishing these transitions, the historical accounts will be shown in bold type like this, and will be introduced and concluded with the symbols ► ◄.

Sections displayed in italics represent, for the most part, quotes copied directly from other historical sources. They include in many instances, the accounts of the pioneer individuals who experienced the wilderness firsthand. I want to emphasize, however, that these are not exceptional stories; they are typical of what most pioneers experienced and endured.

At the beginning of the book, you will find a map of the entire Looking Glass watershed. Following that are six river section maps to assist you in following the journey and narrative, and to locate points of interest and of historical events along the river trail.

Readers are encouraged to contact the author with any corrections, helpful additions, or other suggestions.

Author's contact: tbreusch@comcast.net

Other books by this author:

The Story of Aral, Benzie County, Michigan: ca. 1870 – ca. 1922. Available from info@benziemuseum.org.

Ancient Forests: Trees and Timber in Bible Lands and Times. Available from www.schulerbooks.com.

ACKNOWLEDGEMENTS

I thank my gracious wife for sharing the river ride with me, as well as for her enduring patience, and for covering for me in my neglect of other duties, as I pursued the writing of this second book. Thanks to my kids: Jayne, Tedd, Todd and Christina for their love and appreciation of nature, which I was then happy to encourage and share.

I very much appreciated the helpful information on places, structures and events surrounding the ghost town of Glass River, as it was shared with me by descendants of long-time family residents of the area, in particular Sheriff Brian BeGole, Mike Steele, Linda Wright, and Elizabeth Howard Poe. It also includes Duane Tune, who paused his spring planting of soybeans, stepped down from his Massey-Ferguson, and pointed out a number of evidences of the past community.

The staff of the Shiawassee County Historical Museum in Owosso also diligently searched for pearls of information regarding Glass River.

A special thank-you to the gracious and helpful descendant families of Duane and Lucy Babcock for the recollections and clarifications relating to their family's history on the river. They include: granddaughter Irene (now Dunham), age 109; Sharon Shumaker, great-grand daughter; William, great grandson, with wife Estelle; and William Jr, great-great grandson.

Volunteer staff of "The Archives of Clinton County Historical Society" dug deeply and earnestly into files and drawers, finding documents which shed light on early property ownerships and family memories along the river.

Joseph Pulver, Managing Director of the Clinton County Road commission, and Brent Friess, Managing Director of the Shiawassee County Road Commission, both assisted with questions regarding legal road and river access, bridge construction and bridge histories in their respective areas.

Brad Gurski, Director of Operations of the Southern Clinton County Municipal Clean Water Facility provided explanations and reviewed my summary materials regarding operation and design of the facility, as well as the operation of stormwater drains.

I am indebted to the staff of the Nokomis Learning Center in Okemos, who located information and materials, and especially to Alphonse Pitawanakwat, specialist in the Anishinaabe/Ojibwe language, who led me to the meaning of the original native name for the Looking Glass River.

Thanks to Mark Ward, long-time riverside resident, for sharing with me his recollections of river water levels and quality over the last several decades.

Of special note is Jeanne Bewersdorff, who identifies herself as an "educational advocate," a role which she fills admirably with her awesome knowledge of area history, and which she readily shared with me, either directly, or through numerous valuable leads and suggestions. She is a very active member of the Portland Area Historical Society.

Gloria Miller, founder and long-time president of the Friends of the Looking Glass Watershed Council, offered her stories and counsel regarding several historic incidents related to the river. She is a life-time resident of the watershed, and a powerful advocate and volunteer for its protection and responsible use. She was particularly inspirational in the pursuit of this project.

Thanks to Darren Lash, Schwan's delivery agent, who told of his personal viewing of a cougar in the watershed, as well as the experiences of one of his customers on his route within the watershed.

I appreciated the special efforts of Wayne Summers, who helped to track down the probable original site of "Indian Green," and to Kenneth Coin, DeWitt historian, for providing many of those and other clues.

Kelcie Sweeney, Executive Director of the Clinton Conservation District, diligently searched for and successfully located a digital copy of the Looking Glass River watershed, and generously offered its use.

Lt. Thomas R. Wanless, State Boating Law Administrator, Law Enforcement Division, Michigan Department of Natural Resources, provided guidance and explanations relative to legal navigability of Michigan streams, and for the legality of accessing rivers from public road rights-of-way.

I am so very appreciative of the generous time and efforts offered by Gloria Miller, Larry Arbanas, Jeanne Bewersdorff, and Kerry Orr, as well as my daughter Jayne Nitz, and wife Bonnie, for the assuredly tedious review of my manuscript for accuracy of descriptive and historic commentary, for clarity and content, and for many other very valuable suggestions. Any remaining errors or misstatements, however, remain my full responsibility.

My thanks to David M. Brown, author of *The Michigan Atlas*, for allowing me the use of his fine maps, which I used as the base for denoting the points of interest and historic locations along the route.

Thanks to all of the un-named members of the Friends of the Looking Glass River, who do so much for the river and its users, and several of whom personally helped and encouraged me in this effort.

And finally, I say "thanks" to my patient and accommodating kayak partners and car spotters, to make the physical portion of this adventure a reality, and to share in my enthusiasm. They included wife Bonnie, son Tedd, daughter-in-law Jessica, son Todd and grandson Carter.

And let us not forget all those hardy pioneer families who followed wilderness trails and rivers, and carved out farms and villages in the middle of nowhere. Thanks to them for sharing their stories, and to the historians who foresaw the importance of saving those stories before they were forever lost. Without them all, there would be no Looking Glass River story.

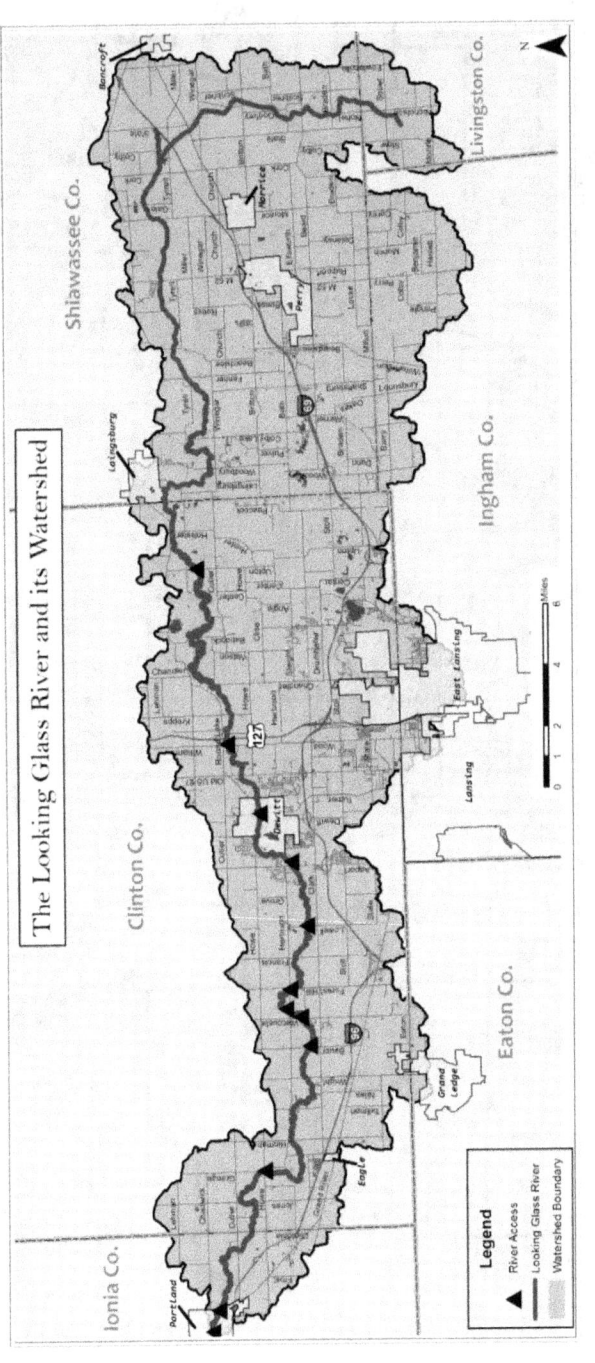

Watershed Map courtesy of the Clinton Conservation District, St. Johns, Michigan.

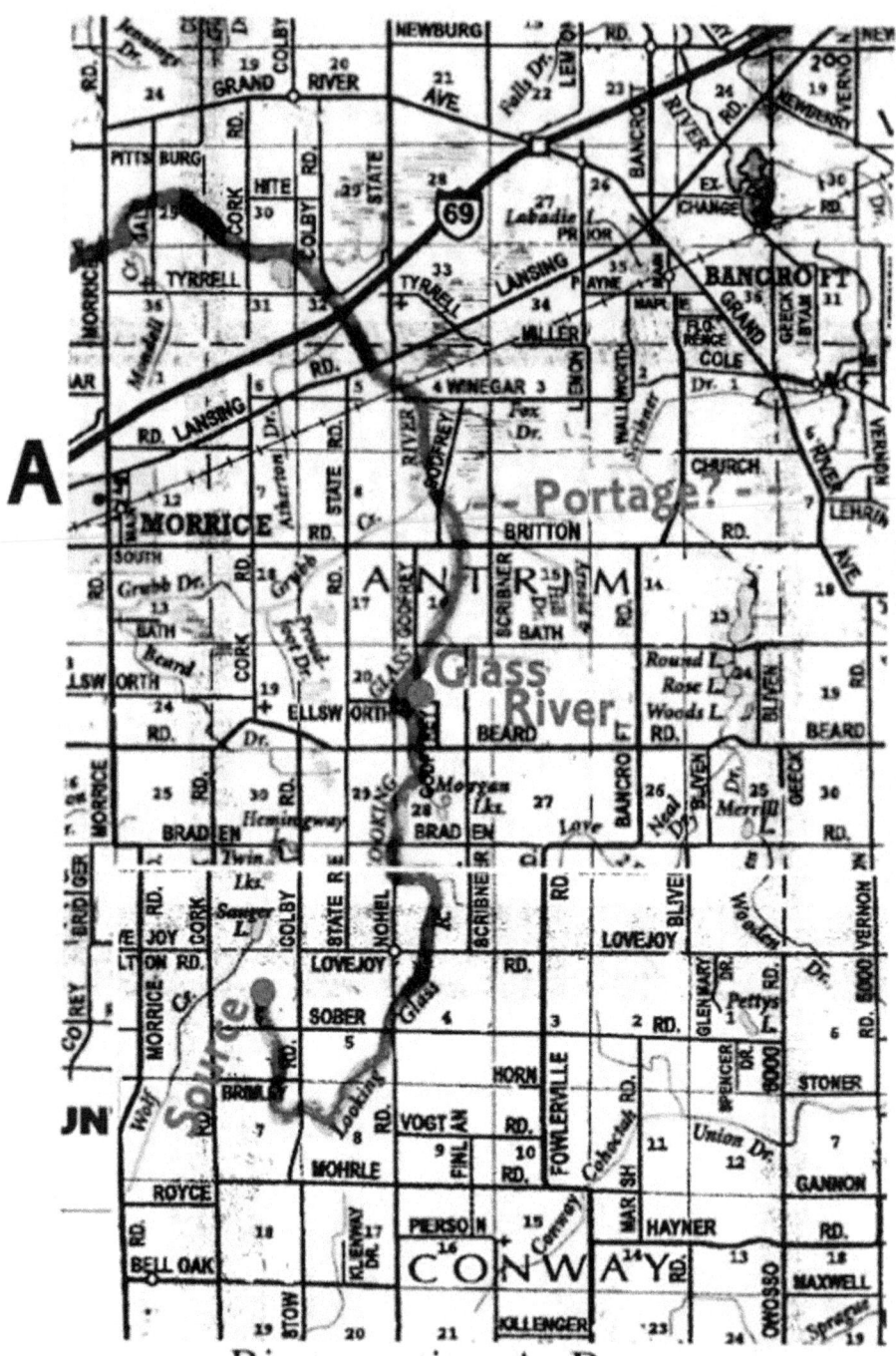

River section A. Base map courtesy of Michigan County Atlas.

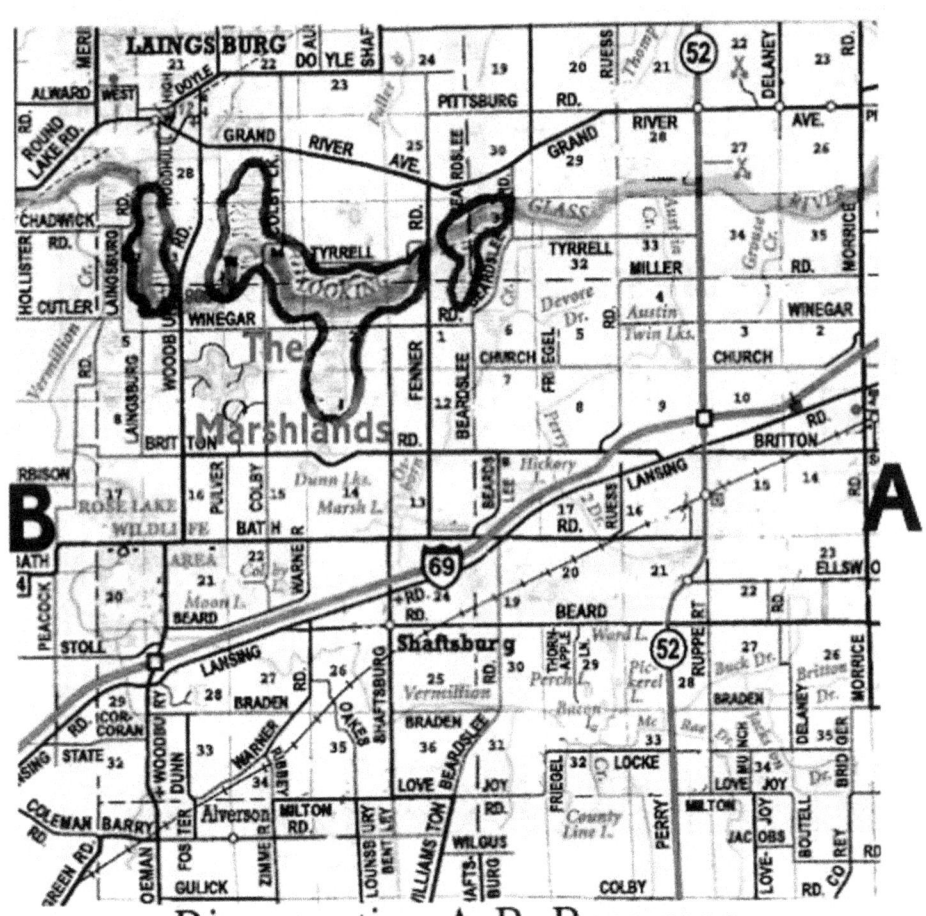

River section A-B. Base map courtesy of Michigan County Atlas.

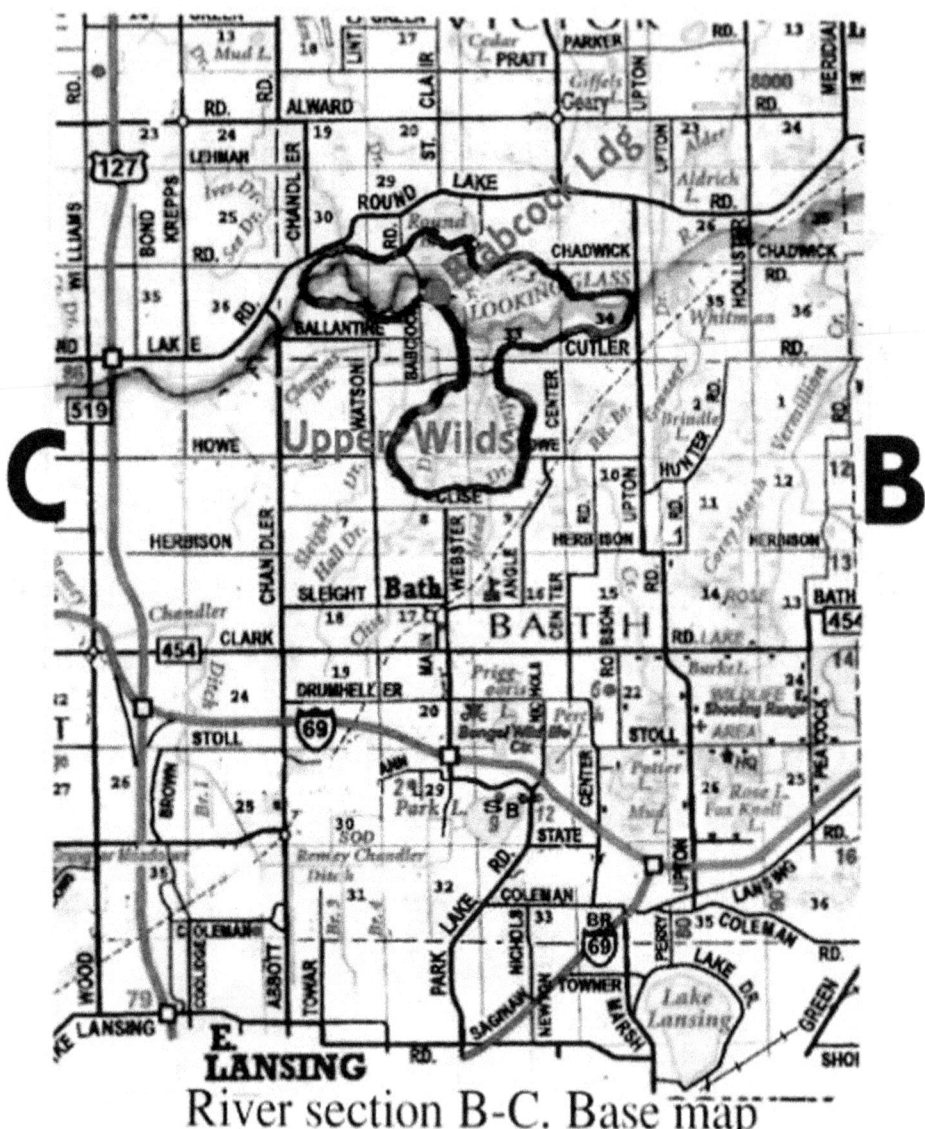

River section B-C. Base map courtesy of Michigan County Atlas

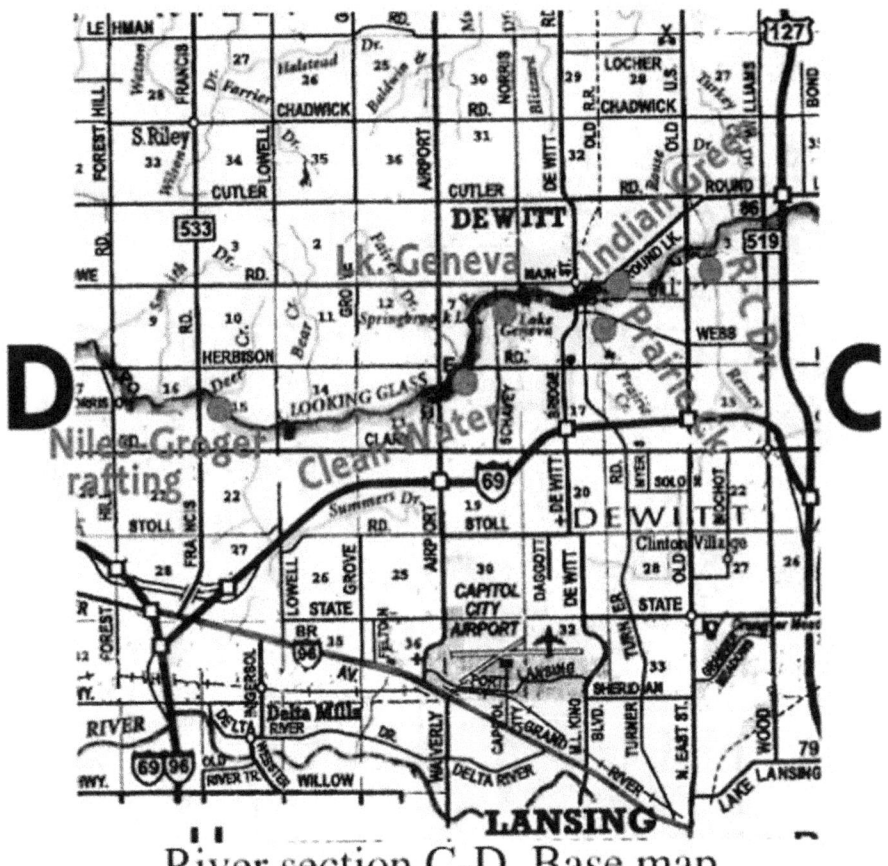

River section C-D. Base map courtesy of Michigan County Atlas.

River section D-E. Base map courtesy of Michigan County Atlas.

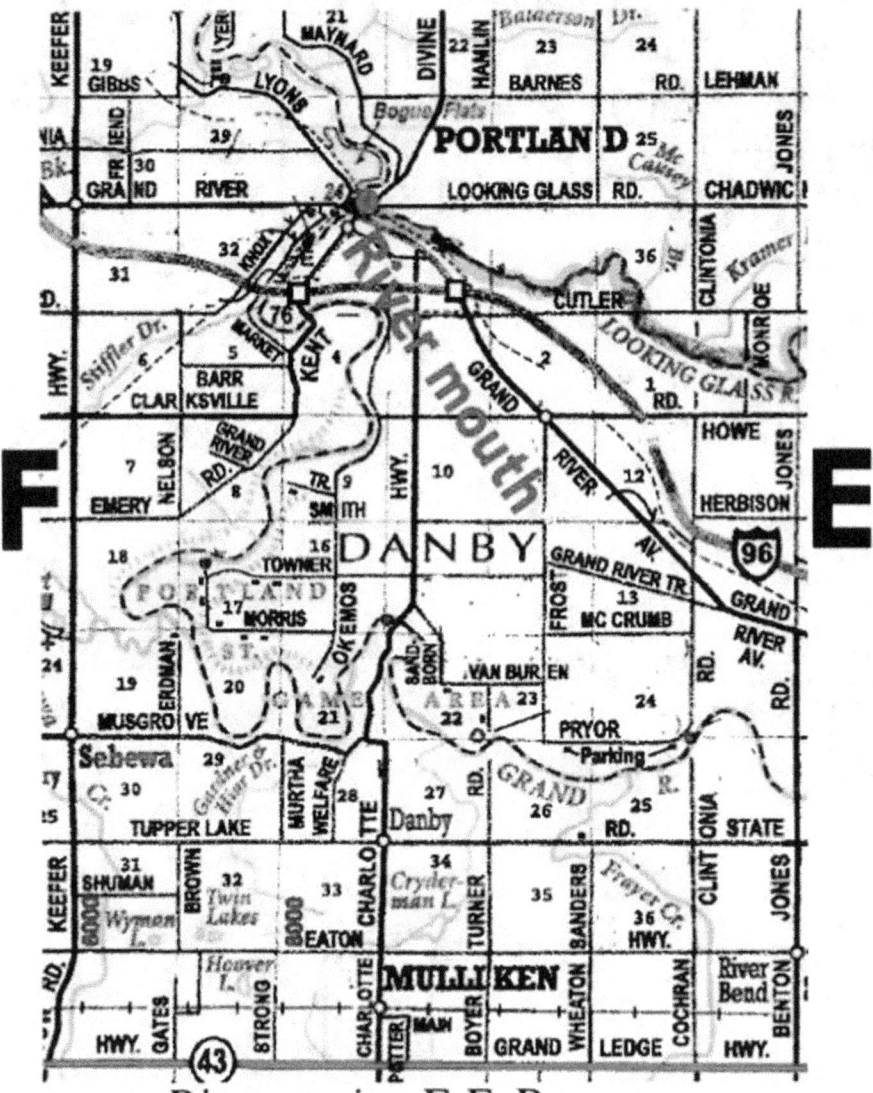

River section E-F. Base map courtesy of Michigan County Atlas.

✶ THE DREAM ✶

    I have always loved the outdoors. I grew up in the country about five miles south of Holland, Michigan. It was farm country, but we lived on a small lot adjacent to my grandparents, and they owned 18 acres that was in the process of reverting from farmland back to woodland. This gave me lots of land on which to roam – and I did. With my three brothers, we enjoyed a sand hill, a raft pond, a fishing hole back by the railroad tracks where steam locomotives once passed, and mixed field and woods. Here I pretended adventures, made a map of all the interesting natural features, and built trails, little wooden bridges and a tree house.

    Exploration and adventure were in my blood. I sometimes thought I had been born too late, and would have thrived on journeys of discovery with the mountain-men, French voyageurs, or western migrants in their Conestoga wagons. I would have liked to be among the first to discover a new valley, a secluded lake or waterfall, a mountain peak. But, given my all-too-practical nature, it wouldn't have worked out. I didn't really have that kind of courage, and by age 21, I was a married man, and less than a year later, a family man as well. Such adventures would have been irresponsible to my wife, Bonnie, and new daughter, Jayne.

    However, my interests had carried through to my choice of forestry as a career goal. I selected Michigan Technological University, where incidental to my studies, I was also able with fellow forestry students to explore lots of backcountry in the wilds of Houghton County, to check out old copper mining sites, and to hunt deer and grouse in unlimited woodlands. Following graduation in 1964, I was hired by the Michigan Department of Natural Resources as a forester. In this capacity

I was able to spend a great deal of my official work time in the backwoods of Michigan's state forests, the largest dedicated state forest system in the entire country. My own favorite activity was called "Operations Inventory," which required information-gathering treks into every part of my assigned area of state forest. It included some of the most wild and remote areas of Leelanau, Benzie and Manistee counties, even back to the origins of tiny streams in the depths of very large swamps. While out gathering forest data, each such trip was my version of a westward exploration during expansion of our country, away from roads and any signs of human influence, and never sure of what might be coming up next.

Often, many of our family vacations were also planned to include adventure, whether by backpacking, camping, hiking, canoeing or just poking around in some of Michigan's small wilderness areas. Michigan indeed has numerous and wonderful opportunities for enjoying the wilds first-hand, yet without substantial risk of life or limb. Of note, it boasts nearly 5 million acres of state and national forests, 101 state parks, 7 national parks, more than 15 dedicated wilderness areas, over 35,000 miles of streams, and 11,000 inland lakes. In addition, the private sector offers hundreds of fabulous opportunities to enjoy nature-based activities. Adventure simply awaits the adventurer!

And just what do I consider qualifies as a worthy "adventure?" Well, it's time away from home and civilization, pursuing some single- or multi-day activity out in nature. Generally, it suggests inclusion of some kind of special effort, challenge or endurance. Yet on the sensible side, something with a reasonable and definable beginning and end, either in activity, distance, time or any combination.

With my wife, sons and daughters, brothers, or extended family members I have trekked and camped the Pictured Rocks National Lakeshore, The Porcupine Mountains Wilderness State Park, the Pigeon River State Forest, the Sand Lakes Quiet Area, the Jordan River Valley and North Manitou Island. We explored the interior of the Sturgeon River Gorge Wilderness and the Rock River Wilderness. I canoed short sections of a few wild rivers in Michigan and Wisconsin, and in Lake Mijinemungshing in Ontario's Lake Superior Provincial Park. And there were plenty of much simpler outings such as bike rides on wooded trails, day hikes, camping in many of Michigan's state parks, enjoyment of National Parks from California to Maine, and no end of beautiful and rugged scenery in so many places.

Eventually some complications developed. A pinched nerve in my back made it vulnerable to pain. I developed neuropathy in my feet making it somewhat uncomfortable and unstable to walk any great distances. Or over rough terrain. Or with a pack on my back. I tore my Achilles tendon in my right foot when searching for big trees in retirement and although repaired, it remained quite stiff and further hampered extensive walking.

At age 74, it was obvious that my stamina, strength, and moderate aches and pains would no longer enable me to carry a 40-pound backpack or walk long distances. My wife and I turned in our big, heavy canoe for a pair of kayaks. This opened new "doors" as we could now carry lighter craft, and given that kayaks sink only a few inches into the water, there is only minimal effort to propel it. This also provided more opportunity for accessing the upper reaches of tiny streams and marshes and to explore remote areas where others with deeper conventional watercraft were unable to go. This had great appeal! The opportunity for exploration and adventure had returned in another form.

But, in addition to these partial-day kayak trips in many parts of Michigan, I had begun looking for a longer and more defined kayak "adventure." I wanted to find something with a definite wholeness about it, and preferably not far from home, so that it might be accomplished in reasonable and convenient segments.

Michigan's Looking Glass River seemed like a natural. There were no dams - it was all free-flowing. Portions of it were just four miles from my home. I even lived within its watershed! But there was another compelling reason. In browsing the several books on paddling in Michigan, available in our local library, only one even mentions the Looking Glass. And that one is deliciously titled *Michigan Rivers Less Paddled*, by Doc Fletcher. I suppose that distinction stems from a number of reasons: shallow water – especially in late summer, narrowness, frequent tree blockage due to irregular maintenance, slow current, and only a very limited number of formal points of access. Only one canoe livery was located on the entire river.

Yet, whatever the characteristics contributing to its low usage, to me that was just a stronger beckoning and an added delight for those very reasons. The river begins in Livingston County, the first of six counties through which it passes in its 70-mile journey. I was anxious to begin at its precise origin, or at least as close as possible. Such was my dream.

✷ THE SOURCE ✷
WHERE DOES THE RIVER REALLY BEGIN?

The *Looking Glass RiverTrail Guide* begins its river description and trip suggestions at the Upton Road bridge crossing. But Upton Road, in Clinton County, is some 40 river miles downstream from the proclaimed source of the river in Conway Township of Livingston County. So, I needed to look much farther upstream in my search for the ultimate source of the Looking Glass River.

UNDERSTANDING WATERSHEDS

Just what defines a river's source? Perhaps this is a good place to introduce the concept of a watershed. A watershed is all of the geographic area drained by a particular river system. It is the common area within which every drop of rain which falls, if it were to travel unimpeded in a "downhill" direction, would eventually reach that particular river, and be carried down that stream until it ended and merged with another larger body of water. For the Looking Glass River, its "end" is at the city of Portland, where it joins the much larger Grand River, and loses its individual identity.

The border, or fringe, of any watershed is the high line of land between one watershed and another. A drop of rain just to one side drains into that watershed; a drop of rain just to the other side drains into the other watershed. In reality, of course, rain does not flow unimpeded over the surface. Some does, but much seeps into the ground, moving in a "downward" direction underground, above impervious layers of clay or bedrock within "aquifers." These are also the source of water for our wells. Eventually the aquifers emerge as a spring or seep which flows into a small tributary which eventually joins the main river. Over its full length of 70 miles, the Looking Glass River is fed by over 100 additional miles of smaller tributaries and feeder streams, together draining a watershed area of 312 square miles!

*****

With that in mind, let's get back to locating that uppermost source. As one would travel upstream from a river's mouth, many tributaries are adding water and increasing the volume of the river proper. At these stages, it is not very difficult to distinguish which is the main river and which is the tributary. The river itself clearly maintains the greater width and the greater volume of water. As the actual upstream source comes nearer, however, even the water in the main river diminishes to a trickling stream, and now its tributaries begin to look of similar size. Before the days of airplanes and overhead satellite photos, it would have been hard to tell which small tributary constituted the main river. In fact, it would often have been the mapmaker who either intentionally or unintentionally made the determination. In the absence of other evidence, the longest feeder stream was commonly and logically given the distinction. But even this was not easily determined in a largely unsettled wilderness.

These early difficulties are evidenced with the Looking Glass too. The 1840 *Gazetteer of the State of Michigan* indicates that the Looking Glass River has its origin "in a small lake in the southern border of Shiawassee County, flowing first northerly." This interpretation is probably not surprising, and can readily be understood from a glance at the Shiawassee County map of today. A short stream does originate in Section 32 on the south edge of the county between State and Nohel Roads, flowing from a tiny lake that is today more of a large marsh. It flows northerly. But it is also obvious today that this is only a tributary stream and that a greater flow of water comes from the stream it joins, and that is actually the main branch.

The issue had still not been satisfactorily resolved by 1875. The *Atlas of Livingston County*, published in that year, does show the main thread of the river reaching south into Livingston County, but then heading directly west, ever so slightly into some wetlands of Ingham County's Locke Township. The 1895 atlas corrects this error and shows, as most maps do today, the river instead bending back to the north in a short loop, in the marshes still within Conway Township, and all within Livingston County.

The whole concept, however, became more complex when later many "county drains" had been constructed (more on these in a later chapter). Then it was up to the drain commissioners as to which routes, which natural seeps, often not even very conspicuous, were to be dug out to produce an actual flow out to the main channel. These actions often, in effect, extended the "river" up ditches and into farmland.

This problem remains evident even today, as a 2016 map of Michigan counties shows the Looking Glass extending farther south into Conway Township. A closer look at current topographic maps shows how this may have happened. At one point county drains from opposite directions essentially drain the very same farm field located east of Stow Road. Some extend northerly to form the Looking Glass which we are following, and the other drains southerly to the Red Cedar, as does Wolf Creek just a little farther west.

*****

And so, on the morning of December 28, 2016, my wife, Bonnie, and I decided to begin our examination of the upper reaches, finalize the source, and determine the potential navigability of the Looking Glass River. While this may seem a strange season in which to begin, several things made this day a good choice:
- it was predicted to be sunny, always a plus for outdoor adventures, especially after the run of cloudy days Lansing is famous for;
- a warmer forecast than we had experienced for the last couple weeks;
- the absence of summer leaves, which would make peering upriver or into the initiating marshes much easier;
- a quick recent thaw of 10 inches of snow, which would send maximum water down the waterways – presumably similar to the highest waters of spring runoff – and make them easier to spot;
- and – oh yes – general cabin fever.

Having already studied the maps and satellite views of the upper reaches, we set off. Our first destination was the "apparent" source, which we hoped to satisfactorily identify and then follow downstream, both for descriptive purposes and to determine at what point it became navigable for our kayaks during the following summer. The map and the satellite view both promised that this starting point would be near Sober Road, Section 6, this being the extreme northwest corner of Conway Township, Livingston County.

We approached from the north via North Herrington Road, noting as we got close that while the land was essentially flat and nondescript, here was obviously the ever-so-slightly, yet highest plateau of the area. Even this gravel road was nearly contiguous with the adjacent farm fields – no ditch or slope at all separating the two. The same was true on Stow Road, one mile to the east. This was evidence that there was no real water flow of any kind here, and that the many marshes we encountered were virtually stagnant.

Well – almost. Gravity, of course, will do its thing, and the highest plateau of an area forms the sources of all streams. The Looking Glass seemed to draw its first drops of water from here, as we would soon try to demonstrate. Still, caution was advisable. Not more than a mile away to our west a drain which would become Wolf Creek drew its water from the marshy areas around Sauger Lake, Twin Lakes and Hemmingway Lake, all situated upon this same plateau. Yet Wolf Creek sent its water southwest to join the Red Cedar River in its own separate watershed, and then went on to join the larger Grand River. Obviously, we were right near the junction, the fringe, between two adjacent watersheds. To further demonstrate the complexity, just two miles in the other direction, to the east, falling raindrops would move eastward to join a third watershed, that of the Shiawassee River, thence to the Saginaw River, and then Lake Huron! Between the two, the Looking Glass would flow north and eventually westward within its own separate watershed and after 70 miles join the Grand River, which would eventually empty into Lake Michigan.

While many streams have their origin in small spring-fed lakes or ponds, numerous others begin in simple marshy areas or wetlands. Such was to be the case with those of the Looking Glass. In fact, now narrowing our search into the area about a half mile east of North Herrington on Sober Road, we passed what topographic maps of the area showed as the highest point in this area at 930 feet above sea level. As previously pointed out, the land tapered downward in all directions from this point. And so, just beyond we reached a very narrow swamp of lowland hardwood trees which gave evidence of the stream's origin just to the north side of the road. Its present appearance was simply as small, shallow pools of standing water, but of course there was an as-yet imperceptible movement of water southward into a similar stand of trees on the south side of the road.

As our intention was to track its route and growth, we next proceeded to drive the nearby roads to each of its crossings in a downstream direction. The next point of interest was Brimley Road. Between Sober and Brimley, the satellite photos show a number of very distinct and larger treeless marshes, all oriented in a north-south direction, and already gathering additional water. A tiny culvert had been placed under Brimley Road at this point. The culvert gathers the water from the open marsh visible on the north side of Brimley, and funnels all of it out the other end. This very tiny flow, although only one-foot-wide, is the first real evidence of the Looking Glass River!

From here, it flows southeasterly through a wooded area, exiting a quarter mile later in a farmer's open crop field. It then turns easterly, crossing Stow Road less than a half mile south of Brimley. But its look has changed! The flow has increased to a width of one to two feet, and all of it is now clearly confined to a very straight and narrow "ditch." Its appearance east of Stow is similar, running easterly through another farm field, in a line as straight as an arrow.

※ THE WHAT AND WHY OF COUNTY DRAINS ※

Within not much more than one mile of the river's source, the promising narrow wetland drainage and small marshes had already been funneled into a straight and narrow ditch. Obviously, this was not as nature had designed it. So what happened?

▶ Sometime after 1800, trains of covered wagons pushing westward became increasingly common. They were in search of cheap new farmlands and new lives for an increasing number of immigrants and families becoming more crowded in the developing East. Many passed rather closely by the southern border of Michigan Territory, yet failed to select Michigan as their new home. By 1810 there were barely 4,000 White inhabitants, and Native Americans still held technical title to most of the Territory. The War of 1812 with Great Britain stifled progress as well, but it also drew attention to the value of its water ports.

In addition, major Indian treaties acquiring land for the United States government began in about 1795, and continued into the early 1800s. That affecting most of the Looking Glass River Watershed occurred in 1819. Soon after acquisition, government surveys were begun, first in the more populated southeastern Michigan, and subsequently in other ceded areas. Once they had become officially registered, such lands would become available for purchase by settlers.

But along with this arose another "issue" which would negatively affect Michigan as a destination. The surveyors almost immediately encountered numerous lakes, wetlands, bogs and marshes, a great hindrance to the exacting nature of their work. These unpromising encounters were also incorporated in their official government reports, and so for a time the survey work was put on hold. Territorial Governor Cass, however, had faith in Michigan's future, and convinced the federal authorities to resume the surveys. While the surveyors began to also encounter rich soils and vast forests, unfavorable reports of more swampland discouraged prospective settlers and farmers.

Detroit, founded by the French in 1701, was among the earliest settlements in Michigan, and the water port and entry point for many commercial interests, military excursions, and eventually would-be pioneers. Given that the southeast part of the state was in fact lower, flatter, and wetter than the rest, it is not surprising that the early observers obtained a poor impression. Perhaps the earliest and harshest report to that effect was given by the French Baron La Hontan, who traveled the Detroit River and Lake St. Clair in 1686. He recorded that in his opinion, the entire region was "the fag-end of the world," that term meaning the absolute farthest end of anything!

Even later, formal commentary by some high officials cast doubt on its potential. The following report was sent in 1814 by General Duncan MacArthur, who was stationed at Detroit:

> *I have no hesitation to say that it would be to the advantage of government to remove every inhabitant of the Territory, pay for the improvements, and reduce them to ashes, leaving nothing but the Garrison posts. From my observation, the Territory appears to be not worth defending ... nine-tenths of the land of the Territory is unfit for cultivation ...*

Edward Tiffin, Surveyor General of the United States, reported in 1815 that based on the reports of his surveyors, sent to inspect the southeastern part of the Territory, Michigan apparently consisted of swamps, lakes and poor sandy soil not worth the cost of surveying. In his opinion, not more than one acre in 100, or perhaps 1,000, would permit cultivation.

As late as 1859, Horace Greeley wrote in the New York Tribune to describe the northern half of the lower peninsula as being

> ... cold and uninviting to the cultivator, diversified by vast swamps, sterile and gravelly knolls, and dense forests of but moderately valuable timber, and not yet readily accessible, so that its settlement was likely to be slow, and its population sparse for generations.

Harriet Munro Longyear, a Michigan settler from whom we will hear more later, related that in 1836 her parents, seeking land to the west, had first checked out lands in Illinois, Indiana and Wisconsin. They had bypassed Michigan initially, because, in her words,

> They had seen "Michiganders," as they were called, returning to the state of New York. Their sallow complexion and the tales they told of shaking with the fever and ague made my father think that Michigan was no place for him.

These symptoms were of course the result of contracting malaria from mosquitos. John Nowlin further relates in his book *The Bark Covered House*, his experiences of the 1830s:

> We had many annoyances, and mosquitos were not the least...and...drove the oxen and cow up to the smoke which we kept near the house in order to keep those little pests away...Many times, in...going through the woods there would be a perfect cloud of mosquitos around me. Sometimes I would run to get away from them...The woods were literally alive with them. No one can tell the wearisome sleepless hours they caused us at night.

Even more specific to the location or our interest, Mrs. M. J. Niles recalled in 1885 that when her family, amongst the first pioneers of the area, were contemplating Michigan:

> Clinton and its surrounding counties were described as a desert of swamps and sand knolls, and grassy lakes, and low, dark forests, fit only to be inhabited, as it was, by Indians and wild beasts and snakes.

But how bad were conditions, really? Information compiled by the Cass County Drain Commission shows that Michigan had been ranked as the 5th wettest state in the nation. The criteria? The nature of its soils, abundant rainfall totaling 26 to 36 inches of rain per year, and topography in southern Michigan which was largely flat. In fact, pretty much all of the Lower Peninsula east and south of Isabella County was included within the heading "major land areas with drainage needs." That's the major part of 26 of the Lower Peninsula's 68 counties, and the first areas which would have been encountered by would-be settlers moving west and north. ◄

*****

Time and first-hand experience would soon demonstrate, however, that these were overstatements of the negatives, even though they aptly described some of the difficulties, and what would be a very real problem in effective farming – lands too wet to cultivate. The government was determined, of course, to paint a brighter picture, and to remedy whatever deficiencies it possibly could, so as to encourage continued and more rapid settlement, and progress toward statehood. Ditches constructed to drain away some of this standing or near-surface moisture were deemed to be the answer. Among the reasons touted in their support were to protect public roadways, to reduce some of the flooding from storm water runoff, and of course, to make more farmlands tillable and other lands developable. Public health issues were another great concern, especially as it pertained to the miseries surrounding malaria, known to be transmitted by the mosquitos thriving in such stagnant lowlands. Understandably, settlers were fearful in their investigation of Michigan as a potential new home. Removal of these intimidations and impediments was essential to encourage settlement and utilization.

Again quoting the Cass County website, "Among priorities of early leaders was creation of a system of roads promoting access to interior regions. Our first Territorial drain law, enacted prior to 1820, provided drainage for these early highways," rendering a drier and firmer base to support its horse-drawn wagons laden with heavy household goods. Of course, once arrived, these same pioneers required tillable farmland able to support the weight of a team of draft horses. And so, the report continues, "Subsequent laws led to the draining of rich upland marshes and swampland for crop production. To a growing population it had become apparent that extensive systems of artificial drainage were necessary for continued expansion of agricultural and related activities." The first state drainage statute was passed in 1839, with numerous revisions over subsequent years as the population and activity increased. John Nowlin concurs with the associated benefits, as he states later in his book: "We had them (mosquitos) many years, until the country was cleared and the land ditched; then, with the forest, they nearly disappeared."

*****

These days it would be difficult to travel a mile of road within any of the southern Lower Peninsula's farm country without crossing a county drain. On the upper reaches of the Looking Glass, perhaps no segment is more representative of the look and results of a such a drain than the previously-referenced area just to the east of Stow Road. Clearly dug by man within a previous natural drainageway, it is perfectly straight and of uniform width and depth. The water flows swiftly and free of brush and obstructions. It carries water from "upstream," which due to the ditching is now better able to seep out from under the adjacent and otherwise waterlogged farmland, and thence to be more promptly carried away, leaving the land firmer for farming activities.

As Bonnie and I drove the roads crossing these upper reaches of the watercourse, however, we found inconsistency in the degree of creation and maintenance of these "ditches." In general, where the course ran through lowland wooded areas, the course either had not been cleaned out, or had begun to revert. In the more open areas, with adjacent pastureland or cropland, the straightness of the course and resemblance to a "ditch" made the intervention of man evident. Many of the first miles of the Looking Glass that we examined met that description.

Joining the main river from both sides, many more, shorter county drains flowed into the main river all along its early route. In Shiawassee County alone, at least 412 open drains are recorded, rushing water off to not only the Looking Glass, but also the Shiawassee and Maple Rivers. Downstream in Clinton County a similar total number of drains have been installed, and in Ionia, still about half that number. Often drains were named after original settlers, perhaps on whose farms they were originally dug. Here in southern Shiawassee, for example, they included Peck, Morgan, Clay, Griffith, Scribner, Love and Neal, among others.

In more modern times, subsurface plastic tiling has been installed right out into the farm fields. These slotted tubes further extend the reach of the draining process, adding even more water to the county drains into which their flow is directed.

✳ NAVIGATING THE RIVER ✳

As already stated, my objective was to kayak the entire navigable portion of the Looking Glass. It turns out there are two aspects to the term "navigability." For my own practical purposes, "navigable" would simply mean that my kayak would float freely, and I could avoid numerous obstructions like brushy areas, fallen trees, log jams and even these shallow drainage ditches. Legally, however, "navigability" could be quite a different issue, and that needed to be clarified before I slid my kayak down through someone's front yard and into the river. While Michigan has basically a very helpful interpretation, permitting wide usage of streams by boaters and fishermen, it is far from clear in some situations. Obviously, I would need to find out, or at least be able to make a reasonable judgement.

THE LEGAL ISSUE

Let's look at the legal issue first. The Michigan Department of Natural Resources, Law Enforcement Division, has diligently researched the issue and carefully prepared a treatise on the subject. They also responded to my written request for the latest clarifications. Early territorial ordinances considered many waterways as "common highways," which purpose of course they historically served in the absence of an elaborate road system. This "right" of boating and fishing prevailed on the "navigable," and therefore "public," streams. Enter here, however, the challenge of defining what is public and legally navigable and what is not.

Often cited as the basis for proof of historic commercial navigability is the ability of a stream, in its natural condition, to "float a log" cut by early timber harvesters who sent it downstream to mills and markets, a commercial use. Although courts have periodically struggled with a more precise definition for decades, the commercial use/log flotation test continues as the controlling test of navigability. And the right to fish has been consistently tied to that interpretation.

In the specific summary provided by Lt. Thomas R. Wanless of the Law Enforcement Division:

> *Michigan courts have established the log flotation test as the means for determining whether a stream or river is navigable. See, e.g.,* Bott v Natural Resources Comm, *415 Mich 45 (1982). In Michigan, this test dates back as far as the mid-1800s. See* Moore v Sanborne, *2 Mich 519 (1853). The determination of whether a specific stream or river is navigable under the log flotation test is often decided by the courts on a case-by-case basis.*

In the absence of a specific court determination, or obvious ongoing public use, you will have to exercise caution. Fortunately, a great many of Michigan's streams have been deemed navigable, providing wonderful opportunities for their users.

As it turns out, the matter of legal navigability really wouldn't become a significant issue on the upper reaches of the Looking Glass. My adventure-minded and ego-driven ideal had been to kayak the full length of the river, beginning from an imagined spring-fed pond, from which would flow a small but distinct stream which would immediately be...the Looking Glass River, and would accommodate my kayak. However, I should have gotten a clue when I reviewed the Looking Glass RiverTrail Guide, and saw that their first point of kayak entry listed for a river journey was Upton Road, which as already noted was some 40 miles downstream from the river's source, and only 30 miles from its end at the Grand River in Portland. Did that mean we were destined to skip more than half of the entire river in our anticipated adventure and exploration? Was the guide based on simply a "reasonable" trip for the novice canoeist? Was it based on the belief or knowledge that Upton Road provided the first suitable access site? Were those upper reaches only navigable in the best of high water, and thus not suitable during most of the preferred canoeing season? Had someone tried this before and simply found that the upper reaches were too clogged with trees and jams? Larry Arbanas, long-time river user, in fact advised me that some 20 years ago he had attempted a section beginning farther upstream at Woodbury Road, and encountered lots of downed trees. We soon found out that all of these restraints were applicable over one stretch or another.

*****

Legally floating <u>upon</u> a stream was one issue. Legally <u>accessing</u> that stream with your kayak or canoe from the shore was yet another. Were bridge crossings or roadsides appropriate for entering the river? Some counties seem to feel that carrying or dragging a boat within the road right-of-way, as long as one remains within that 33 feet of center line on either side, is reasonable. Others are reluctant to make such a statement. Lt. Wanless again offers the judgement of the Law Enforcement Division regarding accessing of streams or rivers at bridge crossings:

> *Again, that determination would likely be made on a case-by-case basis. A court would make that determination by considering the nature of the dedication as determined by the intent of the party who dedicated the road for public use. See* 2000 Baum Family Trust v Babel, *488 Mich 145, 153 (2010). However, the Michigan Supreme Court had held that public roads that terminate at the edge of navigable waters are deemed to provide access to the water.* Thies v Howland, *424 Mich 282, 295 (1985). When seeking to access a stream or river at a location other than publicly owned land, the Department of Natural Resources recommends obtaining permission from the property owner.*

With regard to the above summary, note the discussion of the Hinman Road intersection with the river, as will be discussed later under the section on "The Niles Settlement." My personal, not official, impression is that that intersection, at least on the south side, represents a reasonable access down to the river's edge. When considering any access, however, keep in mind as well that parking your vehicle on the road itself, or its shoulder, may be illegal in some places.

THE PHYSICAL ISSUE

With these considerations of navigability in mind, we continued to systematically inspect every stream crossing from its source in our automobile. The only thing consistent about its navigability from a physical standpoint was its <u>lack</u> of consistency. The Looking Glass began as a natural lowland drainage. Within just a mile or so, its identity as a county drain was very evident, and while there was rather significant water

15

flow some 1-2 feet wide, it was definitely not going to accommodate my kayak. The next crossing, another mile downstream at Sober Road, told a different story. The stream was still a drain, but at this point several feet wide, in places overflowed into adjacent lands, and obstacle-free. We were hopeful that this might be our put-in place for the entire rest of the journey. The north/south Nicholson Road crossing was equally promising, a very pleasant kayaking stream, now of 10 feet in width. At the east/west Lovejoy crossing, however, our hopes were jolted, as the stream was now flowing naturally, but swift and narrow, with many quick turns and with occasional brushy areas.

We were now in Shiawassee County, and crossed the stream again at Nohel Road. To our east was a drain, open and about 6 feet wide. For a short while it continued this way to the west, but quickly lost itself it a distinctly wooded area and natural course all the way to the east-west Braden Road. Though increasing in depth, it all passed through a single large culvert here, emerging into yet another stretch of drain through an open field which was here easily navigable. GPS satellite views suggested this would return to a natural flowage before reaching Beard Road one mile north. But our review of navigability was about to be interrupted by an interesting discovery. An 1875 map of the area labels a "mill pond" of considerable size backing up the Looking Glass for nearly half a mile south of Beard. Though the pond has since disappeared, might a navigable channel still remain?

Driving north and checking at Beard Road, now more than 6 miles from the source in the swamp, the view back upstream toward the south again raised some doubt. To the north, while the stream at first appeared very open and navigable, a closer inspection showed that this too was soon overtaken by brush and jams. It entered another wooded area extending all the way to the next crossing at Ellsworth Road. That 1875 map shows in that section a <u>second</u> mill pond some quarter mile long. A little research showed that these ponds were once formed by a dam on the Looking Glass. This too has long since been removed, but obviously we were not going to be able to inspect either pond by kayak. Yet the mill ponds were certainly an intriguing find, and beckoned for a closer investigation.

✳ THE GHOST TOWN OF GLASS RIVER ✳

Standing on the bridge over Braden Road and looking northward in the spring of 1875, the next mile and a half of the Looking Glass River, much unlike today, would have appeared to be an easy kayak trip, wide and free of brush, log jams and fallen trees. The *Shiawassee County Atlas* for that year clearly shows the reason. As noted, two large ponds, labeled "mill ponds," were located here, occurring in quick succession, with only a very short stretch of narrow river in between. Up until these last few miles of following the route down from the river's source through marshes, woodlands and farms, the landscape had remained nearly flat, and the river only slightly below the adjacent wetlands, which would flood every spring. However, as Bonnie and I drove farther along, tracing the developing river northward along State Road, we had begun to notice that the terrain was changing. Somewhere north of Braden Road, it was becoming more rolling. The river began to develop a more distinct and deeper "valley," and its banks on both sides grew higher. This provided the ingredients necessary to construct a dam and use its water to provide a source of power for mill machinery, and to float logs. This asset, as in so many other early settlements, did not go unnoticed.

My first impression was that there may have been a dam and mill of some sort at the head of both of the two ponds. The more northerly, downstream pond had clearly been created by the damming of the river. The other was more questionable. It might have resulted from a second dam located at what is now the Beard Road crossing, as this is the first place where the river's banks are notably higher and closer together. But nothing in the atlas nor in the historic narratives say or suggest anything at all about a separate, second pond, or any additional mill it may have supported. Consequently, it is far more likely that the higher streambank elevation near Beard Road simply limited and narrowed the northerly pond's expansion into adjacent lowlands for a short distance, and that this second pond was really just an extension of the first as the lowlands again spread out just south of Beard Road. The county atlas of 1875 and other available information provide more insight as to that first pond, immediately to the north. But first, let's go back and look at the local events which led to these developments.

▶ The first settlers here in Antrim Township were Allen Beard and his brother-in-law Lyman Melvin, who had come from New York, and followed an Indian trail north into Michigan. They arrived at the cabin of Dyer Rathburn and were there told of lands to the west, which had not yet been traveled by any settlers. Setting out again, they crossed swamps and streams, trekking overland until they found an "oak opening," which they chose as their new home site.

These "oak openings" were often favored by early land speculators and pioneers, knowing that they greatly eased the effort otherwise required in clearing land. While often natural in their origin, being the result of repeated wildfires, Native Americans also conducted burns in their efforts to maintain their values for game and gardens. As further recorded in the 1880 county history,

> *Here upon an Indian Mound, in the midst of luxuriant vegetation and bright flowers, they sat down to rest and refresh themselves; and it is retold that Melvin, who was especially charmed by the beauty of the surroundings remarked that if he lived in Michigan, he wished to live there.*

The location of this opening was about one mile west of the Looking Glass River, and nearby was the site where a village would soon spring up. The year was 1836. The county history goes on to describe their considerable efforts after having made a trip back to Detroit to formally purchase their properties:

> *They returned in July with 3 yokes of oxen, a wagon, a small outfit of farming implements and some cooking utensils. They built a small hut of bark peeled from the bodies of black ash trees. The bark was cut in long lengths, pressed out flat and then leaned against the pole of a tent* (the same method used by local Native Americans). *Marsh hay, well dried served for their bedding. They then prepared their land for autumn wheat and returned to their families until time for planting. They returned with their families at planting time and later built their new log homes.*

The Beard property was on the east side of the current Cork Road, and the south edge ran along the road which would bear the Beard name. He had remarked to neighbors, whose descendants would later recall, that in the early years he would have to ride back all the way to Detroit to purchase plow points and other special supplies. He would eventually accumulate over 500 acres of farmland near this location.

Between 1836 and 1839, the four Harmon brothers also settled in the area, taking up property on the Looking Glass itself, both north and south of what would become Ellsworth Road. It was Daniel Harmon who in 1840 dammed the river at a point upstream of Ellsworth Road, creating this large mill pond and building a sawmill at its upper terminus. It was brother Almon Harmon who upon his arrival in 1836 built a good log house north of Ellsworth, less than one qurter mile west of the river. A few years later in 1842, David D. Adams also bought property on the west side of the river, but south of Ellsworth and the Harmon property. He built a log home in 1848. The Harmon property was subsequently sold to John C. Adams, son of David D. Adams, who still lived just across the road. John built a very nice square brick house on the site in1876. It remains today, though with additions, occupied now by the BeGole family, and in very fine condition. Other families soon followed the early settlers, many finding employment at the mill. Many of the mill logs undoubtedly came from the area farms being cleared, and in turn, its products served the building needs of that same growing local population. Lumbering and sawmills were among the major employers in many early settlements.

By 1848 Dan Harmon had sold the sawmill to Thomas Munger, who in turn a short time later sold it to Walter Wright, who had settled in the area in 1848, and later built a house on Godfrey Road just north of Beard. This house remains, though unoccupied, to this day. His brother Issac arrived in the area in 1852, purchasing a one-half interest in the milling property. In 1855 they decided to divide the interests, Issac taking the mill and power, and Walter the land east of the mill pond.

It is not clear just when or by whom a town site just north of the pond was envisioned and platted. County records of today do not show it in their official documents, suggesting that perhaps the plat was never officially registered. There is some likelihood that it may have occurred at about the same time as the sawmill and mill pond were getting started, and "great things" were anticipated. There is also a case to be made for a later timeline. This is suggested by a number of factors, including the naming of the streets. That on the south side was named "Water," due apparently to its proximity to an already established mill pond. The most easterly was Church Street, but a formal church was not built there until 1876. The most westerly street in the plat was called "Orchard," suggesting fruit trees might have already been established nearby by some of the earliest settlers. Finally, it was in 1868, as we shall see later, that the town was renamed as "Glass River," which might have coincided with the establishment of a new plat. We cannot say for sure.

The town was initially dubbed "Antrim," after the township which surrounded it. It was certainly ambitious and optimistic, including 124 building lots intended for sale! Laid out as a square one quarter mile on each side, it was to have five streets running east/west, and five running north/south. The south side of Main included provision for a "public square," and on the opposite side a "school" lot. Historical records suggest that, for whatever reason, the school was not built on its designated lot. In the earliest days of the village, it appears the children attended at more distant schools which had already been constructed.

The town site had been very purposefully selected. It was adjacent to the mill pond on its south side, and less than a quarter mile from where Main Street crossed the Looking Glass River to the west. Notable as well, the town site was clearly the highest piece of land in the whole area, and presumed desirable for both pioneer settlement, and homesites for workers at the sawmill. Mill Street led directly south, its fill across the wetlands near the river forming the earthen dam. A broad depression still exists in the southwestern corner of today's farm field where horse-drawn "slip-scoops" laboriously dragged up dirt which was then redeposited to form that dam and roadway.

This roadway continued on to the dam, a bridge, and the sawmill, which according to early atlases, was located just south of the river and west of the pond where higher ground existed close to the river. The noted location, however, may have simply been to the mapmaker's convenience, and possibly the mill was actually located over the river itself, as was frequently the case. At that time Mill Street also continued southerly (at least on paper) until it connected with Beard Road. Just north of the dam and mill pond, situated along Mill Street, were several buildings, including at least five barns and a blacksmith shop. This shop and the barns suggest support for the sawmill and board and care of horses used in early logging operations in the area, which provided logs for the sawmill. Typically, the logs would be deposited in the mill pond, where dirt detrimental to the saw teeth would be washed off, and from which the logs could then be hoisted up one at a time into the mill by means of an "endless chain," for sawing into lumber. In addition to its primary purpose, the mill pond served the local children as a swimming hole in summer, and a skating rink in winter.

Mill Street also supported a sawmill store. This store was situated on the small knoll which can still be located today on the west side of the old Mill Street location. Apparently over time it served as residence for various owners, some of whom simultaneously operated under the same roof a general store, and/or post office.

At the same general location, but just a little more southerly, along the east/west Water Street, was a gristmill. Its precise location and source of power is subject to some speculation, but Duane Tune, whose family were long-tine residents of the area, offers this reasonable proposal, drawn both from family recollections, and evidences he was able to discover on-site. He points out a substantial dip in the dam/roadway just a little north of the river location. It connects a marshy area to the east (behind the dam) to a marshy area on the west. He believes this may have been a mill race diverted more northerly of the river itself, in order to access higher ground where the gristmill could be constructed. He is, in fact, aware of a depression representing a probable gristmill site nearby. As reasonable as this sounds, the early atlas of the town site gives no depiction of a separate mill race, even though the gristmill itself is clearly denoted to the north of the river.

As settlers continued to move in, there had been enough activity at the town site to warrant the opening of a post office in 1849 (some sources 1851), in the home of John Near. Mail was carried in and out on horseback, Michigan's version of the "pony express," though perhaps not so rushed. In that same year, a more local log schoolhouse was finally built just southwest of the platted Main (now Ellsworth) and Church (now Godfrey) intersection. It was named the "Near School" in honor of the postmaster. In the very next year, however, it was for some un-recorded reason moved by the power of 18 yokes of oxen to a new site about three quarters of a mile to the south and east, on property which had belonged to the Morgan family on Beard Road.

Early on, the settlers were determined to also conduct worship services, and initially utilized the most local schoolhouse, beginning around 1850. It was organized as "The First Methodist Episcopal Church of Antrim." This served them for a quarter of a century, until a proper church was constructed on the site and dedicated in 1876, with a spire 85 feet in height. An Odd Fellows Lodge had been organized in 1874, and shortly thereafter they had built a meeting hall on the west edge of the town. The Lodge met upstairs, and the first floor was used for township meetings and elections. At the time, the village was still described as "thriving," and the above events would seem to support this. The town was renamed "Glass River" in the spring of 1868, after the nearby river. At the same time the postmaster position, which after John Near's resignation had resulted in the appointment of Allen Beard, then passed to Joseph Blinston (or Blinson), and was taken into the store at his residence just a little west of the river and south of Ellsworth Road. Just behind it there is a large pond.

Local recollection is that this building was previously the sawmill store/post office, which had been moved there from its prior location on that knoll on the west side of the farm lane (previously Mill Street). After Blinson, J.C. Adams took the position around 1880.

In spite of the prevailing enthusiasm at that time, the town did not prosper as its planners had hoped. Although the ponds, mill and nearby supporting buildings were still shown as in place and operating in 1875 (and into 1880), that atlas still shows only three or four other buildings within the Glass River plat. Three of those structures were located along the north side of Main Street. The more westerly one was the Odd Fellows Hall. A final dwelling was located just east of Church Street.

The town regressed rather rapidly after this. Records show that the post office was discontinued in 1888. The 1895 atlas shows the mill ponds emptied. While no specific reason is on record, Linda Wright, descendent of onetime sawmill owner Walter Wright, has suggested that railroads may have been the cause. Duane Tune, another long-time resident of the area, concurs with this conclusion. While railroad locations were a boon to towns on their chosen route, they were equally a death knell for many of those bypassed. This suggestion seems to suit the situation at Glass River very well. Here's that story.

*****

It was 1836 when Josiah Purdy built a cabin between what would become the intersections of Main and Gale Streets of Morrice. In 1838 he was joined by William Morrice, and while others followed, settlement of the specific area was very slow for several decades. All of that changed when in 1877 the Chicago and Northwestern Railroad company completed a line between Lansing and Flint. Stations were selected at what would become Durand, Bancroft, Perry, Shaftsburg and of course, Morrice. Morrice had been officially platted as a village just the year before. It now began to grow rapidly.

The timing coincides well with the beginning demise just three or four miles to the east at Glass River. Other contributors to the decline were likely related to a lessening supply of wood for the sawmill, and/or diminished need for the products of this and the gristmill. Typically, as such an enterprise thrived, so did the town. When it regressed, the town followed suit. Today, only one house remains on the north side of Main Street in the platted square. The house just east of Church Street also remains. The building which had also for a time served as residence of Joseph Blinston, early post office and general store, was for a time occupied by Charles Beard, descendent of original settler Allen Beard. It is now painted green and still stands, though vacant and greatly deteriorated. The church was moved to Flint, where it is on display as part of the "Crossroads Village and Huckleberry Railroad." There is no current evidence or indication that any of the streets north or south of Main Street were ever developed. And the only remains of Mill Street's access to the saw- and grist-mills is a narrow two-tracked trail accessing a local farm field. There are a few rock piles and depressions here and there which may mark the location of other structures.

A cemetery remains at the top of the hill just south of Main near Godfrey, where the school and church once stood. It was officially recognized and overseen by the township beginning in 1880. However, it was in use well before that time. A cemetery inventory performed recently by Diana Dempsey indicates that the oldest gravesite was occupied in 1856, shortly after the area's development had begun. A total of 17 people were interred here during the time the post office was active. As of today, many other area residents have been and continue to be laid to rest here, including many from the historic Wright and Adams families. The one-time village remains a pleasant and historic site above the Looking Glass River, and is now an unincorporated area referred to as "Antrim Center." ◄

❋ INTO THE MARSHLANDS ❋

► Before continuing on with our close inspection of river navigability, I should point out that just two or three miles downstream from this historic Glass River site there was once a Native American village of considerable size. There are several such sites of occupation along the length of the river, either as semi-permanent "villages," or seasonally transient "camping sites." This particular site is a logical location for a village, being both at a junction of several Indian trails, and near the likely portage between the Looking Glass and Shiawassee Rivers. While I would like to have known more, and to check out the precise spot, this site was abandoned prior to 1831, and the book *Archaeological Atlas of Michigan* cites the location as "Vague." So instead we must be content to focus on the rest of our river journey. ◄

*****

It was another outstanding sunny day in late February. With the temperature climbing into the 60s, we were drawn to continue our examination of the next downstream portions of the river for navigability in the upcoming spring and summer. Driving onward, the next crossings at Ellsworth, Godfrey and Bath Roads once again dampened our spirits. Although a promising and pleasant waterway, 10-12 feet in width and flowing mostly within natural channels, too many brushy areas and downed trees were still apparent which would make a kayak attempt a potential nightmare. We continued to find adequate water, but similar obstructions were obvious at each road crossing nearly all the way to Laingsburg. There would be occasional long stretches of clear paddling with only a few obstructions, alternating with other stretches of inviting water with long stretches of obstructions. It really didn't matter which; either way prevented carrying out our kayak journey within this area.

Finally, at Colby Road the stream took on a more river-ly stature, with wide and deep waters, and very few visible obstructions. It was still as promising at the Woodbury Road crossing near Laingsburg. This was finally encouraging, and I hoped we had reached physically navigable waters, as I very much wanted to kayak through the extensive marshy area which I knew was coming up shortly.

THE ROLE OF THE FLOODPLAINS

Because of the obstructions encountered so far, we had already had to pass up several marshes which were of interesting appearance from the satellite maps. Until now, all the way from its source down to Britton Road, the river's course had never deviated more than a stone's throw or two from an active farm field, nor more than a half mile from a road. Relatively level lands, and the work of numerous county drains had enabled any potential farmland close to the river course to be utilized.

The first area in which a change became evident was about a mile north of Britton. The woods and marsh here were roughly 400 acres in extent, a wetland longer and wider than any we had yet encountered. It had been too extensive and too costly to drain for farmland or other development. And for the next fifteen or so river miles, such wetland areas, extending farther and farther out from the river, would become more frequent: 200 acres, 200, 500, 100, 700 and 200. On a river system, these areas are called "floodplains."

As the name implies, a "floodplain" is a level lowland adjacent to a river, where there is little or no riverbank. In times of a sudden influx of water from upstream (spring thaw, heavy rainstorm, etc), much of the excess water overflows, or floods, into these nearby wetlands. Portions of these areas are perpetually wet, and under at least a few inches of water year-round. Such seemingly "worthless" areas need to be explained for the very important positive benefits they serve.

Primarily, floodplains provide a natural place for all of that sudden flush of water to be temporarily deposited and then to drain back out to the river slowly over subsequent weeks, rather than to rush downstream and severely flood and damage developed and occupied areas, bridges and other structures. In addition to avoiding flood damage downstream, working floodplains also absorb much of their standing surface water, recharging the groundwater supply for underground aquifers, filtering it for purity, and effectively recycling waste products and chemicals. By slowing the current, streamside erosion is also reduced. Suspended sand

25

and other sediments would otherwise be re-deposited in the river downstream when the current slows. It is commonly known from research that such deposits are harmful by covering the otherwise gravely or clean river bottom, preventing normal fish spawning and food acquisition.

The county drains that we've previously discussed are undoubtedly very helpful to the farmer by quickly whisking away rainfall and snowmelt which would otherwise saturate soils or "pile up" in adjacent fields. Downstream, however, it can sometimes have just the opposite effect. Although all of that water is being quickly funneled away from these upstream farmlands, the heavier flow of water in the main river channel now by-passes the many natural marshy reservoirs which would ordinarily have temporarily held and then more slowly and steadily released that water to the lower river.

Mark Ward, who has lived on the river for over three decades, told me that based on his observations, the water is darker, and the bottom less visible than in years past. In addition, the water level in the river has been averaging deeper in the last six or seven years. Gloria Miller and Larry Arbanas, both long-time residents of the area farther downstream, agree with this observation. Mark notices more dying and blowdown of trees as they are now forced to deal with deeper water adjacent to the stream. He believes a contributor may be stepped-up cleaning, deepening and widening of existing county drains. In addition, in more recent times there has been a rapidly growing interest in the tiling of farm fields even more distant from the river. Perforated plastic pipe has been buried under an enormous acreage, and is continuing at a rapid pace. This underground water is directed downhill to, of course, the nearest county drain and then the river. Of further note, the water and sediment also carry with them all of the fertilizers and other soil treatments used on farm fields. Mark made it clear to me that he was not being critical of county drains or of farming, but rather that we all have to be aware of the side effects of our actions, and take all reasonable precautions and particular care of this treasured resource, the Looking Glass River.

✳ THE LAINGSBURG VICINITY ✳

I should point out here that the volume of water, while important, is not the most limiting factor in traversing the entire route of a river. Since it only takes a few inches of water to float a kayak, more troublesome are the downed trees and log jams which actually block the river. And as our observations have already revealed, these are very numerous in the upper reaches that we've already passed, where the river is very narrow and trees and bushes are growing closely along both banks. After this experience, I must conclude that the Natives of the land must have performed at least some degree of regular river clearing and maintenance. Otherwise, the river would shortly have become of little use to them.

Such efforts had been applied in these modern days beginning at Upton Road, where the "Friends of the Looking Glass River" organization and their volunteers had regularly maintained passage down the river. We had hoped to squeeze in a couple extra miles in advance of Upton, but the spring of 2017 was unusual. Several stretches of very wet weather kept the Looking Glass extended over its banks and out into adjacent wetlands, making kayak travel unwise and delaying our start. Another factor also caused some concern and apprehension. In April, winds of 50 miles an hour blew for an entire day. We lost a tree in our yard, and many others elsewhere blew down. It was almost a certainty that we would find many trees fallen over into the river, and potentially blocking our path. And finally, as we approached the end of May, it became evident that the volume of water flow in the upper reaches had now dropped dramatically following a dry spell, making floating a boat there totally impossible.

One section of river we would consequently not be able to visit first-hand was that marshy area near Laingsburg. For the past few miles the narrowed river corridor would again have offered glimpses of nearby farmlands. It would also pass within just one mile of the heart of the past and present city of Laingsburg. At least one source tells us that at the very same location as this existing city there was once a Native American village called Wassololo. This apparently dates well back to the 1600s, but what happened to it in later years has not been determined.

From all appearances, modern Laingsburg does not owe its origin directly to the river, but more indirectly to the well-traveled and paralleling Grand River Trail. It was this Indian trail, one of the most significant and important in Michigan, which was followed by many westward-bound pioneers, including the popular segment which tracked the Looking Glass

River. Peter Laing settled there in 1836, and shortly built a tavern along the main route to accommodate the travelers. It was very popular and assured the growth of the surrounding village. Eventually the trail became a busy stage route crossing Michigan. The typical sawmills, gristmills and many other businesses and professional offices also took hold along the route, assuring the survival of the village.

✷ "LIONS, TIGERS AND BEARS" ✷

As pointed out earlier, as the river approaches Laingsburg, a number of larger floodplain marshes appear in the landscape. But the most extensive wild and remote area, which I had been anxiously anticipating ever since this journey was contemplated, was still just ahead. And that <u>would</u> be navigable. After just a couple more miles of nearby farmland, the river reaches the potential put-in site on Upton Road, as recommended in the RiverTrail guide. That meant we were about to finally launch our kayaks, and begin that first section of our journey. Before doing so, however, let me provide some further description of this general area. I will cheerfully call this "the Upper Wilds" of the Looking Glass River corridor. The adjacent and previously intermittent marshy and wooded areas will become more continuous, and occasionally as much as a mile wide. Satellite maps reveal that at its core we would be surrounded by nearly three square miles of largely undisturbed nature, and I liked the feeling! It's one which the early explorers and pioneers must have regularly experienced. It would be beautiful in its own secluded way.

These features also make the area suitable for a great variety and number of plant and wildlife species. In Michigan, wetlands now comprise less than 15 percent of its surface area, yet they support half of the state's threatened, endangered and special concern plant species. Around 100 different kinds of birds have been confirmed as utilizing the Looking Glass River watershed, many of them expressly because of its isolation and the large area of associated wetlands. Up until the late 1800s, it would have even included the abundant passenger pigeons, but these had been decimated by uncontrolled hunting and habitat destruction. Among the animals we may now readily encounter are the ones with which Michigan residents are already quite familiar: the beaver, muskrat, mink, coyote, fox, squirrel, opossum, racoon, badger and many others. It also includes a vast variety of both common and rare reptiles, insects, crustaceans, mussels, turtles and other lifeforms. Fish species include panfish, carp, northern pike, rock bass, sucker and smallmouth bass in most sections of the river; bullhead, largemouth bass and yellow perch in certain areas upstream of DeWitt; crappie in the upper portions; and channel catfish at Babcock's Landing. You might also come across an occasional bowfin, dogfish or other species.

THE WHITETAIL DEER

Another very common occupant is the whitetail deer. Bonnie and I have surprised them on numerous prior occasions, and because they are not quite sure what this strange "thing" is just quietly floating on the river, it is often possible to approach them much more closely than would otherwise be possible. They seem to like the deep woods and marshes bordering rivers where human traffic is much less likely than on the uplands.

During early pioneer days, deer were widespread throughout the state, but not particularly numerous due to the widespread forest cover which is not as conducive to producing deer food. As time went by, the heavy logging and regrowth in the early years of the 20th century led to heavy concentrations of deer in the northern parts of the state. My father, along with his brothers-in-law, were among those who annually packed their gear and headed for the Upper Peninsula. They would wait for hours for their turn to board the car ferry at the Straits before the Mackinac bridge had been built. Where I grew up in the country of Allegan County, ring-necked pheasants could be seen by the hundreds in farmers' fields in the evenings. But I was surprised and tremendously excited when I spotted my first deer running across the property in the early 1960s. That situation was similar in other parts of southern Michigan at the time, where sightings had remained relatively rare. Yet today they have increased so vigorously as to be a nuisance to some landowners, and are a source of nearly 50,000 car/deer collisions in the state every year.

THE BLACK BEAR

This area of wider floodplain and wooded river corridor which we would soon enter also entertains the prospect of some rarer and more elusive animals. Larger carnivorous mammals would find this to their liking. Just what else might be lurking there?

The black bear has never been absent from Michigan, and many early settlers were fearful of their presence. In the fall of 1836, the first settler in the area of present Morrice, near a tributary of the Looking Glass, a Mr. Josiah Purdy, was regularly bothered by bears attacking his family's pigs. As a consequence, the Purdy household was said to usually have large quantities of both bacon and bear meat on hand for local Indians and passers-by. Betsy Webber (nee Munroe), another early settler, who resided in the western end of the watershed not far from Portland, made this report about a visit she paid to her sister at the school where she was the teacher. It was about 1838. "On returning from another visit to the school, a huge bear lay in the road before us, who being frightened at our approach, gave a ferocious sound and made a hasty retreat."

After civilization, however, the incidence of bears retreated northward, and for many years its range was restricted largely to the Upper Peninsula (U.P.) and the northeastern Lower Peninsula (L.P.). Only in more recent times have its numbers increased, and its range expanded farther south. I recall the day in the late 1960s when I was a forester for the State in Benzie, Manistee and Leelanau counties. The forest technician serving with me, Clark Oliver, excitedly related one day that a logger had told him of seeing a black bear in Benzie county near the Homestead Dam backwaters. This was highly unusual.

Bears are not communal, and need lots of territory per individual. When, in bear opinion, it gets too crowded, they begin to search out new, less occupied territories. Over time this expansion reached some of the more southern tiers of counties, at least on an intermittent basis, as they wandered in their explorations. Grand Rapids reported a number of sightings around the end of the 1900s.

Our particular area of interest, the Looking Glass River watershed, had at least a couple of wanderers at about the same time. On Friday, May 28 of 1993, a DeWitt Township police officer reported sighting a 200-pound black bear on State Road between DeWitt and Airport Roads. This location was less than two miles west of our house. And, not knowing it at the time, my wife Bonnie, daughter Jayne and grandson Matthew bicycled this very same stretch of road the very next day!

There was another sighting just three miles to the east of there in June of 2005. Judged to be a 2-year old, the bear had showed up near the Granger Landfill on Wood Road, this time just a mile and a half east of our home. A few days later it was spotted again in the Walmart parking lot of the Eastwood Towne Center, a popular shopping mall. I had shopped there the following day!

Each of these sightings occurred along the southern edge of the Looking Glass River watershed. So we should not be overly surprised to encounter a black bear within the watershed, though by their nature they will avoid humans whenever possible.

Overall, the black bear is now thriving once again. The Michigan Department of Natural Resources estimates that today there are about 9,700 bears in the Upper Peninsula, some 2,100 in the northern Lower Peninsula, and still others in the southern Lower Peninsula. Most notable, the population in the northern Lower Peninsula has risen by almost 50 % since the year 2000. But they are increasing most rapidly in the 10-county area from the Leelanau Peninsula down to Muskegon County. Certainly we should expect more of them to wander south and east.

COUGARS?

Compared to just a few decades ago, there is also a greater variety of other species within the watershed. In the March, 2013, issue of the DeWitt Township Newsletter, I was quite surprised by an included article by the "Friends of the Looking Glass River." It stated, in part, "The watershed is home to a diversity of wildlife ... Residents and river users have recently begun reporting the return of river otters, beavers and cougars to the Looking Glass River watershed." I was incredulous! Beavers? Yes, I'd seen evidence of their tree felling. River otters? OK, hadn't seen any, but quite believable. But cougars? Wait a minute! Here in Lower Michigan? Here, just 25 miles from the capital city and the Capitol building?

I dashed off a letter to the "Friends," concerned that this unlikely report would strike fear inappropriately into residents and users of the area. Quick to come to the defense of the report was Bob Bishop, closely associated for many years with the watershed program. He stated emphatically that sightings had been reported which appeared quite credible. He even went so far as to share with me a video clip of an alleged cougar in southern Michigan. It was a rather distant photo across a farm field with a woodsy background. But, it certainly had the appearance of a cougar to me as well.

Was this reasonable? I decided to do some further research, and began with the 1994 book, *Endangered and Threatened Wildlife of Michigan*, edited by David C. Evers. Evers and his fellow writers pointed out that the cougar once roamed <u>all</u> of Michigan. But that had changed over time. Factors affecting the distribution of the cougar and some other wildlife began with the settling of Michigan in the early 1800s, and included cutting and clearing of the forests, plowing of prairies and oak openings, unmanaged hunting, draining of wetlands, payment of bounties, urbanization, wildfires, and other human impacts. In that process, we had also caused the local extinction of bison, elk, wolverine, caribou, marten, and fisher. Humans treated some of these, like the cougar and wolf, as competitive to their interests, or as dangerous. Cougars were wiped out by the early 1900s. Some species have been reintroduced or found their way back from neighboring areas. The latter appears to have been the case for the cougar, and although highly unlikely, a few small remnants just "might" have managed to hide themselves from residents for a couple hundred years, and to eventually expand and be noticed.

More recent information was collected and presented in a 2001 report titled, *The Cougar in Michigan: Sightings and Related Information*. It was prepared by the Michigan Wildlife Conservancy, which maintains an office at the Bengel Wildlife Center, itself located within the watershed. While recognizing the obvious original Upper Peninsula populations, the report also cites early White accounts of Lower Peninsula cougar occurrences in the far southern counties of Washtenaw, Jackson, Allegan, Calhoun, Kalamazoo, Eaton, Mason, Ingham, Montcalm and Oceana. From this list, it is reasonable to conclude that most adjacent and intervening counties also supported the big cat. The writer of the 1906 *Past and Present of Clinton County* tells us that for the earliest settlers of the county, "The wolf, bear and panther had not as yet yielded their possession of the forests and for years would dispute the right of the settlers to invade their domains." But, as noted above, various factors did combine to contribute to its virtual disappearance.

Recently, cougars have been making a very slow, but notable increase in areas of wildland with adequate deer populations. This has included most of the Upper Peninsula, particularly its southernmost counties. It was in 1984 that the first <u>confirmed</u> occurrence of modern times occurred in Menominee County, prompting more widespread reporting by residents and investigations by resource agencies and enthusiasts. Some 50-100 credible cougar reports now occur each year in the U.P. Reports from the L.P. are far fewer, but increasing. Generally, they have favored the large private "club country" holdings and certain other large tracts of wooded lands in the north half of the L.P., mainly north of the Mason to Arenac tier of counties. Yet in 1995 there were reports in Taymouth Township of Saginaw County. In 1999 a family around Flushing indicated a cougar had visited their yard party. In 2004 the Michigan Wildlife Conservancy released a video that showed two mountain lions prowling a Monroe County field. About this same time my brother Don, who resided on the Rabbit River near Bentheim and the Allegan State Game Area in Allegan County, advised me that his neighbor had made a positive identification of a cougar nearby. More recently, Bonnie's brother Boyd told of a cougar sighting reported by a neighbor, just north of his farm on the Allegan/Ottawa county line. There have been reports from Jackson County as well.

I decided to speak directly with one of Michigan's foremost cougar experts, Dr. Patrick J. Rusz, Director of Wildlife Programs with the Michigan Nature Conservancy. These were his comments when I inquired about the possibility of cougar occurrence within the Looking Glass River watershed in 2016:

> *There have been occasional reports of possible sightings within the watershed over the years, though un-substantiated. Based on my research to date, there is very little likelihood of any resident cougars. That means that any occurrence would more likely be a transient wandering temporarily through the area.*
>
> *The closest area where there is documented occurrence of probably at least a few resident cougars is the greater Higgins Lake/Houghton Lake area, with the Deadstream Swamp as its epicenter. Given the free-ranging nature of cougars, especially males at certain times, their travel from this area down to the Looking Glass, a distance of only 100 miles or so, would be within easy reach.*
>
> *In addition, more consistent reports of potential cougar occurrence have occurred in southwest Michigan, even farther south than the Looking Glass. Consequently, movement on occasion through the Looking Glass River watershed is a reasonable possibility.*

Male cougars in particular roam over large home ranges, especially in breeding season, and may travel over 200 miles when establishing new territory. So, is it possible that, like the black bear, there are times when a stray cougar wanders off over several counties and appears for a while in new, and far more southern territories? Favorite foods of the cougar are white-tailed deer, as we've already noted, now far more numerous in the southern counties than "up north." They also eat beaver, rabbits, birds, coyotes, bobcats and other small critters, as well as fish and frogs. All are relatively abundant inhabitants of the watershed.

Male cougars are an imposing sight. Sporting a tawny-colored coat, they average some 7½ feet from nose to tip of tail, and weigh about 190 pounds. They tend to be solitary and secretive, and seem to favor large blocks of undeveloped landscapes and to avoid habitats frequented by people.

So are we at all likely to encounter a cougar, a <u>lion</u>, in the wilds of the Looking Glass River? Likely? No. But I personally find it rather fascinating and intriguing that such a possibility exists in these modern times and highly developed places. You may choose to disagree. I will probably keep my eyes peeled.

✲ ON THE RIVER, TRIP ONE ✲
(Upton to Babcock)

Water, weather and a busy spring delayed our initial float trip, which would be taking us into this wild area. The first day of summer, however, dawned bright and beautiful, with the temperature already in the 60s. It was June 21 and the forecast was clear and dry with a high only into the 70s. It would be perfect for our first day actually on the river!

After spotting our second car down at Babcock's Landing, we came back around to the officially-recommended starting spot on Upton Road where we hoped to find clear paddling. Let me clarify here that Upton Road crossing is <u>not</u> a public access site. Nor are several other of the access points noted on the RiverTrail guide. This means the proper protocol is to ask permission from an adjacent landowner. I did this here and at several other locations, and found the owners very pleased to be <u>asked</u> for permission. Under those circumstances, they were pleased as well to oblige the request; no one refused me.

We carried our two kayaks, each 10 feet in length, and weighing about 46 pounds, down to the river to be loaded with our supplies. We

34

nearly always wear or carry our life jackets, in consideration of the very surprising power of the current. We also bring a snack; it's always pleasant and relaxing to stop for a break on the river. A camera is essential, because you never know what you might encounter unexpectedly! A hat and sunglasses suppress the river's glare. The weather can always change, so we carry a simple rain poncho to ward off light rains. Topo maps of the river corridor help us "see" what is out there beyond our line of sight – nearby roads, extensive swamps, incoming streams, houses, etc. A cell phone is crucial in the event of an emergency, and its GPS feature can give you a terrific satellite overview of your actual position on the river. I would also be taking notes for this story, but I wanted to keep my hands free for paddling, taking pictures and fending off branches. So, I invested in a small digital recorder that was voice activated: off when I was quiet, recording when I spoke. All would be kept in waterproof containers to the extent possible.

    We were ready and anxious to slip into the stream and be on our way. A kayak is pretty stable when sitting down on the river, but getting in can be a little more of a challenge. So, we steadied each other getting in and then were finally off. We had ideal weather, and we hoped the other experiences would live up to our expectations. It was 11 A.M.

*****

    Although we traveled less than four river miles that day, we were not to be disappointed. The river was perfectly smooth, re-enforcing its "Looking Glass" name. This first section was lined with trees over-arching the river. The birds were singing merrily. A dainty iridescent blue damselfly landed on my kayak, and then my hand. They would escort us, or alternately we would transport them, all the way down the float. Bonnie said they reminded her of "little turquoise pieces of jewelry."

    A single very large boulder rose above the water on our left, a surprise and a strange contrast to the fist-sized rocks along the bottom. A great blue heron lifted off from near the shore. We would see many of them on this and subsequent trips, occasionally scolding us with their raucous, guttural cries for interrupting their patient search for food in the shallows.

    Bonnie drew my attention to a wind-toppled pair of trees. Their flat root mat, now standing on edge, faced us. It was clear evidence of their struggle to anchor the tree in soil often so saturated that roots could only survive to a short depth. We also frequently spotted tufts of grass wrapped around low-hanging limbs just above our heads. This was a reminder that at times this river could be 3 to 4 feet deeper!

About a half hour into our journey we spotted ahead a small "jam" which would be our only river obstacle of the day. As we approached to determine a passage, a muskrat poked its head up through the floating duckweed, and then was quickly on its way. The "jam" turned out to be a minor one, consisting first of a slight accumulation of branches, which we easily pushed through. It was followed by a single tree fallen across the river. Although it had broken in the middle, creating a wide "V," the lowest point was still a couple inches above water level. It required considerable effort to scooch our crafts across, being unable to climb out or pull around.

No sooner had we passed this obstacle, and in spite of our vociferous grunts trying to clear it, a doe and fawn appeared straight ahead, walking casually through the tall marsh grasses close to shore. Ahead, two diving ducks slipped under the water and then were not seen again, leaving only small ripples as evidence of their recent presence. A tiny squirrel crossed over the river, nimbly making use of two trees leaning in from each side, and meeting above us in mid-river.

These trees were mostly silver maple, very beautiful in autumn. But we would also see quite a number of willow, some stately tall cottonwoods, occasional swamp white oaks, and a few other species common to wetland areas. In today's section of river, glimpses of civilization were rare and easily overlooked – a small farm field, a plantation of pines - giving a real feel of wilderness to the area. Prevalent adjacent wetlands in this upper river serve to assure preservation of this setting.

We startled a turtle sunning itself on a log, and a few minutes later found a small piece of rare dry land on the left bank. It would serve for lunch. A few pieces of charred wood indicated we were not the first persons to utilize the spot. A pair of dwarf lake iris, Michigan's state flower, shared the site and were the only blossoms we saw this early in the season.

While thus far we had passed by occasional small, open marshy areas, we were now about to enter the largest on the river. Beginning a mile or two above Babcock's Landing, the river spills over into acres and acres of low ground, especially in spring and early summer, and the open marshland grows wider than we would see anywhere else on the river journey. This area is especially favored by the great blue herons and other shorebirds, on high alert as they wait for a small fish or frog dinner. But kingfishers, swallows, woodpeckers, red-winged blackbirds and many others also find it to their liking.

Bright green duckweed was floating everywhere, making it difficult at times to determine where the "real" river flowed, and which route to take. Folks familiar with the river historically report that the amount of duckweed has increased significantly in recent years. While it does best in quiet waters such as the Looking Glass, it is frequently associated with areas of excess nutrients, a form of pollution. And in dense concentrations, it can deplete oxygen and harm fish. The individual plants are very small, consisting of from one to three very tiny leaves and minute rootlets dangling below in the water. To be sure, it is a favored food of ducks. And, in case you are so inclined, humans also eat it in some parts of the world – it contains more protein than soybeans!

*****

It is important to here recall that this day on the river was June 21, 2017. The prior-noted research and references relative to cougars was gathered during the winter of 2016-17, and I thought I would be done with that subject. About a week after our trip, the headline on page 3A of our local Lansing State Journal, read:

DNR confirms sighting of cougar in Bath Township.

The article reported that a Haslett resident had spotted a cougar in his headlights while traveling a rural Bath Township road, and snapped a proof-positive picture. The date of the sighting was – you guessed it – the first day of summer, June 21. The DNR indicated that it was the first time they were able to actually confirm the presence of a cougar in the lower Peninsula. Bath Township is of course within the Looking Glass River watershed, meaning that on that day we had been in the wilds not more than seven miles from a live cougar, and perhaps far less!

Later, on the day the headlines appeared, I mentioned the incident to Darren Lash, our Schwan's delivery agent, who quickly responded that he himself had seen a cougar in the spring of 2016 in the vicinity of the S-curves of Round Lake Road. It was morning and it had simply ambled across the road in front of his vehicle without looking in his direction. He further noted that another person on his route, a resident of the Bath area, claimed to have spotted a cougar in the area on five different occasions! Other folks began reporting their purported sightings to the DNR following the Bath incident, and the DNR is in the process of sorting out which are indeed legitimate.

I guess there is no longer need for further speculation on this issue. And, yes, for the rest of our river journey, I would <u>most assuredly</u> be keeping my eyes peeled!

THE BABCOCK LAKE AREA

Toward the end of that first day's trip, as the wooded shoreline once again poked in from both sides, we approached the site of Babcock Lake, and just before reaching that little lake and Babcock Landing we passed a Michigan Nature Association protected area on the left called "A Looking Glass Sanctuary." It is located on Babcock Road, with the river forming its eastern boundary. Though not identified along the river channel, a sign along the east side of the road, just a little south of the river, states that it is a 14.5-acre sanctuary which they obtained in 2006. It features "southern floodplain forest and associated wetlands, as well as prairie habitat and oak uplands." As would be expected, it includes some rare wetland species. With many protected areas now under its jurisdiction, the Association posts that it is dedicated to "protecting Michigan's exceptional natural habitats and extraordinary and endangered plants and animals."

The area upstream of Babcock was an exceptionally pretty and pleasant area to drift casually, and even upstream propulsion is easily achieved against the lazy current. Babcock Lake is a peculiar phenomenon in that it is a small pond with the river running through its southern edge. The pond itself is really a big bulge in the river that occurs as it makes a slight bend to the left. It is round and surprisingly deep, with its method of formation a mystery to me. My son and I have never caught a fish there, though I know that others have.

At Babcock Road there is an access site maintained by the Department of Natural Resources. It is probably the only site on the entire river which is reasonably accessible for the express purpose of fishing. There is only a parking lot, and the launch is simply the graveled shoreline of the river, so that only small boats can use the area. While not suitable for larger boats or even motors, paddlers are pleasantly rewarded here. It is a popular fishing site, and many boat-less fishermen walk the southern shoreline to cast their bobbered bait or artificial lures into the waters. The area is known for pike, bass, and several other species of - for many - less desirable fish. My son and I have fished for pike both up and downstream, with moderate success for pike, while occasionally connecting with a bass. There is record of a 41-inch pike being taken from somewhere in the Looking Glass, though the specific location was not divulged. If you've never landed a two-foot pike into the tiny interior of a kayak, with a treble hook flashing as it thrashes about, you are lacking a memorable experience. My own memory is vivid, as my son had to cut the barb from a hook which had passed fully through the fleshy part of one finger before it could be extracted!

Be advised that there are occasionally times in the spring when much of this parking area may be under high water. There are also times in late summer when bright green duckweed materializes in patches sometimes so thick as to cover the river and plaster the sides of boats. A sign on site indicates that there are more than a dozen sites along the Looking Glass suitable for access. Babcock's is the second and best, with Upton Road being the first.

▶ **With a road and a small lake both named "Babcock," it is pretty logical to assume that the earliest settler at this location was a Babcock. The Clinton County deeds have no shortage of entries involving "Babcock's" from other locations in that and surrounding townships. The surname also occurs frequently in county history references. All of this suggests a large family tree, and the family was certainly well-represented in the area. E. F. Babcock and N. Babcock established a steam-powered sawmill in 1866 about two miles east of Laingsburg on the Jackson, Lansing and Saginaw Railroad.**

From historic documents, it is clear that the family line associated with the Looking Glass was Duane and Lucy Babcock and their descendants. Duane was born in Massachusetts (another source says New York) in 1823 of father Sam Babcock. At age 21 he married Emma Farmer in Oakland County and visited DeWitt, traveling via the Grand River Trail. Apparently he was favorably impressed with the new settlement and surrounding countryside, and returned in 1848 to claim property in Victor Township. An 1864 plat map shows him as the owner of 40 acres in Section 18, about 4 miles north of the future Babcock Lake. In addition to carrying on farming, he was a cooper and a carpenter by trade, and built many log houses in the vicinity. Sadly, he lost his wife as well as three children rather early. He was married a second time, to Lucy Bugbee, sometime between 1867 and 1870. Lucy had lived just a few miles east on Upton Road. Around that same time, he disposed of his property in Section 18. Six

more children were born to them in subsequent years. In her memoir, Lucy recalls that she:

> *knitted all of the socks and made all of the clothes worn by her family…Roads were narrow and winding and travel was slow, mostly with oxen. A trip to the nearest settlement was a serious undertaking and involved several hours of discomfort…*(and)*…the old Laing tavern where they stopped to get warm after going to town with the ox team.*

Judging from a review of county plat books for the years 1864, 1873, 1896 and 1915, a new road was put in heading south of Round Lake sometime between 1873 and 1896. It connected Round Lake Road with Cutler Road. Deed records for the county show that Duane purchased the property on the north side of the Looking Glass in 1880, suggesting that the road was probably constructed around or just before that time. It was an oddly-shaped parcel – somewhat like a pentagon, reaching the river along its north bank, but running in several non-cardinal directions to the north. It will probably never be clear just why he purchased such a shape, but it did coincide pretty much with a small area of higher ground on both sides of the road north of the river. Everything else nearby in any direction was just more marshland. This was in fact the only reasonable location for another road crossing in the entire four-mile river segment between Upton and Chandler Roads. Perhaps he saw it as potential for some investment or development options. Or maybe he just liked its isolated and picturesque setting. Consisting of only about 18 acres, he did build a house there on the east side of the road. Not surprisingly, the road was dubbed "Babcock Road" (some maps as Babcock Lake Road), and the large pond at the bend in the river was "Babcock Lake." Nearby was what would become "Babcock Landing."

Duane died in 1906, after which his Looking Glass River property was taken over by his son, John. During the early 1920s John purchased 110 additional acres about a half mile south of the river crossing, just east of the corner of Babcock Road and Ballantine Road, and running eastward to the river. On this land, he and his brother Norris, neither of whom ever married, conducted a farming operation. At about the same time, another brother, Duane Babcock Jr. (listed in early plat books as W. for "Wayne") and wife Mabel bought 141 acres nearby to the west on Ballantine, that property running north all the way to the river. Principal crops were rye and corn. They had nine children, two of whom did not survive. Obviously, Babcock Lake was often a favored fishing and summer swimming hole for members of the whole Babcock clan.

One of the children was Irene (now Dunham, and still living at age 109 as of the time of this writing). Irene and her siblings walked a mile and a half to Bath Country School every day up to her seventh grade. After that she attended the Bath Consolidated School. This was the site of the infamous and tragic school bombing by a disgruntled township resident in 1927. Irene's brother was pulled from the rubble having lost part of one finger. A sister jumped from the first-floor window. Irene was spared by a sore throat which kept her home that day. All told, 38 classmates and six adults were killed in the bombing.

By 1940, John and Norris had expanded the farm from 110 acres to 240 acres, now extending northward to the south bank of the Looking Glass, and including both the east and west sides of the road. Much of the addition was wetland, and included the parcel which would some 60-plus years later pass to the Michigan Nature Association. It did, however, greatly increase the amount of his river frontage, running for nearly a mile and a half.

Sometime between 1957 and 1967 that part of John's property located right at the Babcock Road river crossing was purchased by his sister Eleanor (married name Gunther) and her husband. They recognized its potential for another public purpose and at that time it became "Babcock Landing."

As the years passed, Duane and wife Lucy and eventually their five sons were all in turn interred in the Reed Cemetery at Laingsburg. The 1967 plat book reveals that no longer did any Babcock name appear on any property in Victor Township. There was a lasting exception, of course, and that is the road itself, the pond, and the landing. ◄

✳ ON THE RIVER, TRIP TWO ✳
(Babcock to Old 27)

After the reported cougar sighting, we were now somewhat apprehensive, but still undeterred. We re-entered the river below Babcock's Landing around noon on July 5. It was already 79 degrees. Passing under the bridge, the stream is once again constricted to its traditional width, and passes through a picturesque, mostly shaded wooded area. For a short while, it then opens back up into yet another wide and extensive marshland. In times of high water, it covers much of the adjacent area, and some pike hang out there. In low water, all but the river course is an extensive mudflat.

We had now completed our passage through the largest contiguous acreage of woods and marsh still existing in the entire Looking Glass River corridor, some 2,000 acres in size. This is over three square miles, and undoubtedly was even larger in pre-settlement days. An early historian of Victor Township, the southern tier of which we had just traversed, noting the sluggishness of the stream as it passed through miles of wetland, wrote of that stretch, "The Looking Glass River, an exceedingly crooked stream ... affords no power that can be utilized to profitable advantage." No dams or mills in this portion!

The returning shade as we left the last of these big marshes was welcome. Just about at this point, where the wide marsh once more settles back into a discernible river, a large cottonwood towers out over the river. Several years ago, my son Todd and I were fishing this part of the river. Having had no success, we had started kayaking quietly back upstream. Suddenly my son in the lead kayak whispered for me to look up. There on a limb of that big cottonwood, right over our heads, was a bald eagle. It was unconcerned, and so we just enjoyed the moment, and continued on our way.

As Bonnie and I enjoyed this same section on a fine July day, reflections were perfect and persistent, so much so that she remarked that sky and water played tricks on her perception, each being difficult to discern, and giving the feeling of "floating in the sky itself." On the right bank just before the Chandler Road bridge, another large and picturesque cottonwood loomed over our kayaks. There would be a preponderance of such cottonwoods, mostly on the north bank, in the upcoming section.

*****

In the upper waters of the Looking Glass, many stream crossings were a simple culvert or two, reflecting the lesser volumes of water they needed to accommodate there. However, as our journey continued, this had been changing. The Chandler Road bridge is characterized by a flat concrete construction, topped with a familiar galvanized guard rail. This is the typical construction mode in use by Clinton County in modern times. It is described as "side-by-side concrete pre-cast beams on abutments." Henceforth I will simply identify this style as a flat concrete structure. Oh, and as additional assurance of our location, a sign on the side of the bridge facing the river states "Chandler Road."

CAMPING GROUNDS AND SETTLEMENTS

Since the large wooded and marshy area just upstream from here was home to a wide variety of animals and fish suitable for consumption, it is not surprising that another Indian camp, as well as an historic river crossing, had been located here near the Chandler Road bridge. Most likely the area near this bridge was a seasonal camp, its occupancy coinciding with the best times for hunting and fishing in the area. In fact, the original surveyor notes and map from 1829-30 label this as "Indian Fishing Ground." It is of course, like Babcock Road, also the narrowest point in many miles which would enable crossing the river to dry lands on either side.

▶ **According to early settlers, Chief Okemos himself, well known in this area of Michigan, spent time at this camp. Some reports say this is also where he died in 1858. Others suggest it was the Indian village near DeWitt. All agree that he is buried at yet another village which was on the Grand, roughly 10 miles upstream from the mouth of the Looking Glass. It was called Meshimeneconing (Shimnecon, or some sources Mis-she-min-o-kon) meaning "apple orchard," or "apple field." It is now a part of the Portland State Game Area. When the first settlers arrived in this area, that village consisted of some 600 inhabitants. However in 1841, contact with the Whites resulted in a smallpox epidemic in the camp, and some 450 died. They were buried there in their cemetery, and that is where the peoples of Chief Okemos also laid him to rest.** ◀

*****

With little in the way of civilization, Bonnie and I were able to sit back in our kayaks and just enjoy the quiet river. There was an occasional large boulder, some protruding and some submerged. While numerous trees had fallen across the river in the past, previous volunteers had done a good job of clearing out narrow passages. Except for one, that is. This probably recent, small log jam required pulling our kayaks out of the river onto shore and around the obstacle. On the other hand, we made the inconvenience into a pleasant lunch stop. Packing up and replacing our kayaks in the river, we soon needed to skirt the edge of a second jam. There we came across our second sighting of flowers, the white water lily. They were in full bloom, leaves floating flatly on the water's surface.

LOWRY PLAINS

▶ Still another known Indian camping ground was just a mile or so downstream of the Chandler bridge camp, on the south side of the river, at a place later called Lowry Plains. In 1825, John Lowry, seeking better prospects for his family, moved from New York to Michigan. They settled at Lodi Township, just south of Ann Arbor. He did well and among other pursuits, dabbled in land speculation. Consequently, in 1835 Mr. Lowry (some versions spell it as "Lowery") platted 360 acres lying on both sides of the river in sections 1 and 2 of DeWitt Township. As with a number of other very early plats, this one cannot be found in the files of the State of Michigan, Department of Licensing and Regulatory Affairs. So perhaps it was simply never officially recorded with the county. He had some cabins constructed on the south side of the river for sale to early settlers. One of these early pioneers was Dr. Hiram Stowell. Lowry accompanied him to the property, and helped him build his own log cabin. His daughter Olivia recalled the journey to their new cabin after her father had come back to pick up the family in January of 1837:

> *After a night's rest and a sumptuous breakfast* (at their nearest neighbor-to-be), *we were carefully reloaded onto our sleigh for the last three miles of our protracted journey. It was a cold morning – snow deep and no tracks. We were obliged to cross the river on the ice, for there were no bridges. The ice, always treacherous in the Looking Glass river owing to numerous springs along its banks, let one of our sleighs through, doing*

little damage however, except in frightening us, wetting the salt and sugar, and drowning the cat and chickens. It was a short work to reach the house which was built on the river bank for the convenience of water.

A similar experience befell G. H. Hazelton, another traveler along the Looking Glass, traveling by horseback in the winter of 1836 from Ann Arbor to the land office at Ionia. Along the way he followed the Indian trails, which were at times

>...only a bridle path with underbrush cut away. (I took overnight lodging wherever I was lucky enough to spot a settler's cabin. Eventually I) came to a bayou from the (Looking) Glass river, frozen over, which I should be compelled to cross, the ice, as I supposed, thick enough to bear my horse ... Hadn't gone but half way when the whole body of ice went down ... As it went down, it broke into pieces. Springing from my horse and jumping from one cake of ice to another, I was soon on dry land ... (My horse) had a hard struggle, ... however, reached the shore in safety, and we were once more on our way.

*****

The Lowry Plains area would seem to have been a favorable site for John Lowry's proposed settlement, as the surrounding lands are on somewhat higher ground and the river corridor is again narrow. There are today a number of fine homes that have been constructed on the upland south side of the river where the encampment and settlers' cabins apparently once stood or were envisioned.

In spite of today's obvious attributes, in the 1830s the site was not destined for success. From appearances, John Lowry did not personally stick with his venture very long; perhaps it was simply another investment from afar. A deed transfer is recorded on October 19, 1836. The purchaser was David Scott, who had also originated the DeWitt settlement. The deed carried the terms "and appurtenances," and the price paid was $1,720.65 for 344 acres. Both might suggest that some cabins and other improvements were already present. Clearly Lowry retained some association with the venture, as can be seen from his work with the Stowell family, occurring at about the same time as he was transferring ownership.

Whatever the plans and hopes of either Lowry or Scott, they did not work out, and no settlement ever took hold. There is no clear record of just when a bridge was actually constructed over the river at this location. It shows on the 1864 county plat map, but would probably have been in place well before that in order to attract those earliest settlers. The Stowell family abandoned and moved to DeWitt after just four years, and having improved 90 acres of farmland. In either 1890 or 1906 (sources vary), the early wooden bridge had been replaced by a high truss iron bridge. In 1980 the iron bridge and that short portion of Krepps Road on its north side, were both abandoned. A gravel pit, no longer active and now filled with water, provides a picturesque setting in its place. The remains of Krepps Rd bridge which once connected the settlements can still be seen from the river. On the left is a concrete abutment at the river's edge. On the right is a more picturesque cut and fitted stone structure. Both would be easily overlooked if you were not paying careful attention. We will see farther down the river that Scott's venture at DeWitt was by contrast a great success. ◄

*****

After long sections of quiet contemplation, modern reality was about to return. We would soon approach and pass under four lanes of super highway, US 127. We could hear the traffic noises from a long way off. At least we thought they were traffic noises. As we got closer we found it was, surprisingly, the sound of rushing water from the left bank just ahead. Water was tumbling down picturesquely over a wide pile of stones. And the source of such a volume of water? I have no idea, and nothing on a map or satellite view suggests to me an answer. Nonetheless, it was a most beautiful spot, shaded by a big over-hanging maple. It felt again like "up north."

Not long afterwards, the real traffic noises became evident. Just before reaching it, we observed a small bunch of pickerel weed flowers near shore. This flower, widespread throughout the wetlands of America, is characterized by an upright stem topped by purplish-blue flowers, and lily-like leaves, but these were of an emergent (rising above the water) form. We would begin to see a few more a little farther on. We also began spotting some yellow water lilies, also called cow lily or spatterdock. The blossoms were only beginning to protrude from the large buds. Unlike the floating white water lily, the leaves of the yellow version are most often emergent.

We passed under the two bridges of the expressway, each supported by eight enormous concrete beams. The next quarter of a mile on our right was recently purchased by the township of DeWitt, and consists of unusually high ground, some of it reaching very near the river's edge. A canoe landing is eventually planned for this location. This will be a welcome addition, as accesses of this nature are few and far between on the Looking Glass.

The next bridge is at Wood Road, and is constructed just like the one we had passed under at Chandler Road earlier in the day. As further evidence of the location, you could check out (only from the river, of course) the cute little shack on stilts, set at the water's edge on your right as you pass the bridge. A little farther on, we spooked our first Great Blue Heron of the day. Other birds and wildlife were fewer also. This is not surprising, as wetlands typically support greater numbers and variety of plants and animals than do upland sites.

THE REMY-CHANDLER INTERCOUNTY DRAIN

Just before reaching Old 27, we noted six rusty metal posts standing upright near the left shore, and two small metal drain pipes. The metal posts were arranged to suggest they once served as a dock or platform at the river's edge. There was surprisingly little water coming from the pipes, considering that there is quite a bit of water lying just out of our view. Only a very narrow piece of higher ground separates the river from a large pond created during operation of the Boichot Gravel Pit # 2. Just south of Howe Road is another such pond, where gravel operations are still underway.

I knew from prior research that somewhere soon I should be encountering the outlet of the Remy-Chandler Intercounty Drain. I had even previously checked the spot where it ran under Howe Road just to the south, and its flow was significant. But where was it now? We weren't seeing its outlet into the river. I had once thought its course emptied into the pond just over the river bank, but that tiny dribble flowing from the pond outlet pipes didn't match the much heavier volume seen just a half mile away at Howe Road.

So we glided on slowly, carefully searching the south bank. Just beyond the metal posts and drain pipes is a small mowed area down near the river, a spot obviously enjoyed by the owners. And just beyond that was a small island. The main river flow clearly went to the right, while a lesser channel, partially obscured by accumulated logs and branches, went to the left.

I decided to poke my kayak into the left channel as far as it would go while Bonnie waited. And there it was! Much to my surprise, the outlet of the Remy-Chandler drain is a free-flowing creek of considerable volume, and as beautiful a small feeder stream as will be found anywhere along the whole length of the Looking Glass. And contrary to my earlier thoughts, it runs independently of the gravel pit pond, just skirting its west edge all the way to its junction with the river.

*****

Let me point out here that most county drains are placed so as to move water along a pre-existing path of least resistance, that is, using the location of original seepage patterns, and merely digging them out wider and deeper and straightening their course, to increase the flow from the marshlands and lower the water table. The Remy-Chandler is different, and is a special story worth telling.

▶ Up through the early 1800s, the southeast part of DeWitt Township, and the southwest portion of Bath Township were, for the most part, an enormous marsh. By my calculations, its core may well have been as large as three to four thousand acres; one source suggests a total area of some 7,000 acres. That is five to ten square miles! An oddity of the landscape, and contributing to its existence, was the fact that much of the land between it and the Looking Glass was relatively high ground. Hence there was no significant natural outlet draining the area. And so it had remained, in the eyes of many a major detriment to agricultural use of the whole area. What to do?

Zachariah Chandler was born in New Hampshire in 1813. His parents were well-to-do farmers and so, when he became a young man, they offered him $1,000 to initiate a business enterprise. Believing his best opportunities for such a venture lay in the developing edge of the wilderness, he made his way to Michigan. Here he began a mercantile business in dry goods in Detroit. At this he was very successful, by the time of his death being considered among the "millionaires" of the country. His business also took him to the far reaches of the Peninsula, where he was able to meet a great number of citizens and influential people. All of this would eventually prove helpful to his growing interest in political actions which would be beneficial to his adopted State.

In 1851 he was elected mayor of Detroit. He entered the service of the United States as elected senator in 1857, and served three consecutive terms. While losing his bid for a fourth term, President Grant promptly appointed him to the head of the Interior Department in 1875, an experience which would serve him well in his upcoming project in Clinton County. In 1879 his bid to regain his senate seat was successful for another term.

At this time there still remained in mid-Michigan that huge marsh covering much of southeastern DeWitt Township and southwestern Bath Township. The original government surveyor had labeled them "swamp-lands." An early commentator referred to it as "a worthless and malarious swamp." With his usual heart toward public improvements, and an eye for means by which to accomplish it, Mr. Chandler had an idea.

He began by purchasing from a variety of owners some 3,160 acres of these questionable lands. He referred to them as a "farm," a prospect which it was his intent to demonstrate if at all possible. Perhaps it could be drained. He wrote: "Michigan contains thousands of acres of precisely this kind of land ... If this tract can be reclaimed, others can be, and I propose to give the experiment of reclamation a thorough trial." Investing tens of thousands of personal dollars in the project, the main drain was laboriously cut through the intervening higher ground. It perhaps reaches its deepest cut at Webb Road, where the drain is close to 20 feet below the hilltop. Lengthwise, it extends southward and eastward some nine miles, all the way to Park Lake, along with more than 50 miles of connecting lateral ditches.

As the lands of "Chandler Marsh" were successfully drained, they became muck farms, consisting of rich organic matter resulting from the decomposition of large quantities of prior vegetation. Chandler experimented with a variety of agricultural crops, including grazing grasses, corn, potatoes, rutabagas, turnips, oats and others. The farm was also properly equipped with main house, barns and other structures, granaries, livestock, tenant houses and every other useful piece of equipment. As we can all today testify, his experiment was for its time a great success. In more recent years, these traditional crops had given way to sod farms on much of this land. In time, all of this transitioned to other commercial ventures, as notable today by the many Chandler Road apartment buildings, housing developments, supporting commercial buildings, and golf courses. And as well, still some mighty fine farmlands! ◄

*****

Back on the river, as I was busy checking out the exit of the Remy-Chandler drain, Bonnie had been studying the jam of small logs and branches at the head of the island which had hid it. Some had clearly been gnawed off by beaver. We had not seen any of the typical lodges, nor had we expected to. Beavers make two kinds of dens, depending on their environment. Those living in rivers with significant fluctuation in water levels make their dens by digging holes into the river banks. Lodges and beaver dams are not utilized, as the strong spring surge of high water would flood them or wash them away. Such structures are used only in lesser rivers or streams, or in other sluggish waters and marshes. How do they know the difference? I don't know.

We shortly passed four other kayakers resting in a bend of the river, the only other boaters we had seen thus far. For better or for worse, however, and probably some of each, kayak use has been increasing significantly in recent years, particularly farther downstream.

❈ ON THE RIVER - TRIP THREE ❈ (Old 27 to DeWitt)

The bridge that hosts "Old 27" is another flat concrete structure, this time with a guard rail consisting of two dark brown horizontal rails. And again, a green highway sign on the railing facing the river indicates "Old U.S. 27." Now recall that we have already confirmed the presence of "bears and lions" (cougars) in the watershed. Well, on the right bank just after passing Old 27, we finally also saw those elusive "tigers." Well OK, tiger lilies, that is. While not native to North America, the bright orange and black flowers are very prolific spreaders, and are now considered naturalized in at least 42 states. Both up and down stream of Old 27, there were also numerous white Lizard's Tail flowers, mostly along the north bank. They are erect, emergent plants with narrow heart-shaped leaves, and tiny white flowers arranged along an elongated spike, often bent over or drooping - like a lizard's tail. A few buttonbush plants were also seen along this section. They are small woody shrubs, with white flowers arranged in small ball-shaped clusters.

The river then turned southwesterly for a half mile or so. This meant we were finally approaching the city of DeWitt. It is the only municipality located fully on the Looking Glass River. In this area we would begin to see the as-yet highest concentration of development, housing, businesses, other human activity and associated effects. While we await that appearance, let's take a few moments to contemplate the look of this particular area a couple hundred years ago.

USE BY THE NATIVE AMERICANS

Water Trails and Indian Green

▶ Along the river, we have already passed a number of Native American villages and camping sites. As we here approach within about a mile or so of the modern-day city of DeWitt, just try to imagine that so far on this journey you have seen no evidence whatsoever of human civilization. Then look up at the north bank of the river and imagine an active Indian village. Only about 175 years ago, you would not have needed to imagine. It is the site of "Indian Green" (or Village Green), the third of about five known villages or camping sites along the length of the river. Historians know that there were more than these, but are not sure of their locations.

The 1880 *History of Shiawassee and Clinton Counties* provides this description of Indian Green:

> *There was still in existence at that time* (first settlers) *the Chippewa village of Wabwahnahseepee* (sometimes spelled Wabwahaseesee or Wabwahnaseepee or Wabwahnahsupu or Wabwahnasupu or Wabwahnohseepee) ... *This village was broken up soon afterwards ... though the place continued to be for many years a favorite ground for the temporary wandering parties of the Chippewa bands.*

Perhaps it would be more accurate to suggest a declining, but still purposeful seasonal use of the area for a time, such as gardening, hunting and fishing.

Some of the generalized early descriptions would seem to place it at about the point where the river's short southwesterly course again turns west. However, judging from conventional maps and satellite views, and after drifting this section of river in our kayaks, we found that the north bank near this bend consisted of wetlands for some distance back from the river. It would not have been a great choice for access to a popular camping ground. On the other hand, just a little farther upstream, around a half mile downstream from Old 27, the high ground comes down close to the river's edge. It seems to me that this would be a more likely location for Indian Green. It is about due south to southeast of the DeWitt Grain Corporation silos on West Round Lake Road. Perhaps it had been located on lands now occupied by the Innovative Industrial Park or the adjacent spacious home sites on the pleasant hilly upland to its west nearer the DeWitt city limit. Some suggest it may even have been as close as the present site of the DeWitt City Hall.

Or, the city itself. The account of David Scott's arrival in the area indicates that:

> *There were at this time three families of Indians living on the banks of the Looking Glass River, where the pretty village of DeWitt now stands.*

And, a poem written later in her life (1887) by Miss Mary Foreman, early settler in the DeWitt area, reads:

> *Here stood the lodge of the red man, now moved far away,*
> *on the ground DeWitt Village is standing today.*

I should mention that there is another source which has applied "Indian Green" to a location a little farther downstream at the present McGuire Park. It indicates that these riverside flats were an Indian garden site. However, my own conclusion, shared by other local historians, is that the camping ground labeled "Indian Green" was a site slightly to the east side of DeWitt, as early sources refer to "up" the river from DeWitt, and "above" DeWitt, in river terminology. This area was also a more upland and dry site suitable for living. The McGuire Park site, on the other hand, is flat lowland adjacent to the river. Both the rich soils and ready access to the river for watering during dry periods make such a location very logical as an associated garden site. Separated by only about two miles at most, travel between the two sites – garden and village - by either canoe or the north-bank Indian trail would have been a simple matter.

*****

It should not be at all surprising that all of this activity was focused along the river. Native American life was closely tied to the essentials and benefits which water provided. Consequently, the majority of Indian settlements were established along waterways, and very few actually lived in the dry inland areas of Michigan. Favored areas for their main villages included the mouths of rivers, river crossing places, and portage areas.

So here they lived and here they died. There are a number of "burying sites" on the banks along the Looking Glass. On the other hand, there is very little evidence of actual burial <u>mounds</u> on the river, except near where it joins the Grand at Portland. Some indication has also been reported on the west bank of the river off Airport Road. However, more than 60 mounds have been found in other locations in Clinton County, mainly in the valley of the Maple River to the north. That is, in fact, the second greatest concentration of mounds in all of Michigan.

The rivers themselves made natural travel routes for canoes. As we've already noted, in southern Shiawassee County, a mere three to four-mile overland portage brought the Natives from the Looking Glass over to the Shiawassee River, which eventually accessed Saginaw Bay and Lake Huron. Working downstream on the Looking Glass led to the Grand River, and eventually to Lake Michigan.

Foot Trails

But even more extensive than these naturally occurring water routes was a network of overland foot trails, which connected all of the important sites, and most river systems. The trails were essentially well-worn paths established by centuries of travel – the Native equivalent of the roads and highways of today. Early surveyors crossed and made note of many of them, as well as villages and garden plots, as they surveyed the southern Michigan Territory. The paths connected not only the villages themselves, but also their farming sites; sugaring places; gathering areas for fruits, nuts and berries; seasonal hunting and fishing sites; widespread and sometimes distant locations for buying, selling and trading goods with other settlements; or simply visiting with relatives and friends.

Often such trails paralleled the heavily-used river corridor. Locally, the east-west travel route along the Looking Glass favored the north edge of the river. This was the obvious choice when one examines the feeder streams and wetland locations. They are more expansive on the southern side, which would have made it more difficult for travel on that side of the river. Following it in an easterly direction, the route eventually intersected a major north/south trail from the Straits southeastward to the area of Pontiac and Detroit. Heading west it led to the mouth of the Looking Glass at Portland. A separate branch of the westerly route passed through Pittsburg and Laingsburg before veering off cross-country near Round Lake to join the Grand River near Lyons/Muir, then following the Grand down to Lake Michigan. Large parts of this route are approximated by today's Grand River Road/Avenue all the way from Detroit to Grand Rapids. There were numerous other branches and routes. As more settlers moved through, they improved many paths by marking the routes, locating alternates around swamps, constructing crude bridges, locating stream fording sites, and making similar improvements for themselves and those who would follow.

The Source of Essentials

In those days, as we've already noted, before the advent of the white man's clearing and draining, nearby wetlands were more common and expansive. These sites supported an abundance of black ash (*wiisgaak* in the Native tongue) and white birch trees, and these were especially valuable to the Natives. As we looked up toward Indian Green before 1830, we would have seen numerous shelters, or houses. Contrary to popular depictions, most southern Michigan Natives did not live in tipis (teepees). Rather, the typical shelter here on the Looking Glass would have been a *wigwam*, or *hogan*. In Michigan, it was not necessary to move entire camps at frequent intervals – they were at least semi-permanent. They were constructed by cutting numerous green and pliable young sapling trees which were in plentiful supply, and bending and tying them together at the top to form the frame. The contributors to Wikipedia.org provide this description:

The domed, round shelter...(with)...curved surfaces make it an ideal shelter for all kinds of conditions. These structures are formed with a frame of arched poles ... which are covered with some sort of roofing material ... Some of the roofing material used included grass, brush, bark, rushes, mats, reeds, hides or cloth. Men built the wigwams and the women put on the coverings.

As noted previously, bark of both the black ash (before the modern emerald ash borer invasion), and the white birch (before extensive clearing of the last century or more) were used. Wide strips from the entire circumference of a section of either type of tree were readily separated from the trunk when spring sap began to flow. They were then fastened to the frame in overlapping layers, like large shingles. Animal hides could be used instead or in addition. Brush, dried grass and hides could form comfortable beds.

Narrow strips of black ash wood were typically made into fine carrying baskets. After black ash logs had been stripped of their bark for covering their dwellings, the inner section of white wood was pounded to loosen the annual growth rings from each other. Then, starting at one end, a cutting tool began by slicing the width of the desired basket strip for a short distance from the log end. By more pounding, prying, and pulling, several layers of annual growth rings were simultaneously pulled up from that end to the other. When fully separated from the tree, they represented several layers of suitable basket strips. Moving over another width on the log-end, another section was forcefully pulled up from the log, and so on until the entire circumference had been pulled free. They were then woven into a variety of useful sizes and shapes to serve their needs. Originally serving various personal uses in their daily chores, some were very decorative, and eventually became popular with incoming white settlers as well. Birch bark (*wiigwaas* in the Native tongue) was also favored for use as containers for gathering, cooking and storage, even of liquids. The bark was formed up into a squarish bucket shape, and the joints sewed together with basswood or cedar strips or other natural cord, and then sealed.

Strips of white birch bark formed the basis of canoe coverings, but many more species of trees available along the Looking Glass were also part of the canoe-building process. <u>Birch</u> bark was separated from the tree much as the black ash was. <u>Ash</u> or <u>cedar</u> from the swamps or the river's edge formed the framework and supports. Where necessary, they were tied together with strips of <u>basswood</u> bark. After framing around the cedar, the bark sections were sewn together with small roots of the local <u>spruce</u> tree, pulled from the ground. Gum collected from the <u>spruce</u> tree was processed with animal tallow to use as a sealant for the seams of bark to render it waterproof, yet flexible. Early settlers also noted that some canoes were constructed as dugouts, each carved from a single tree. Obviously, with processes such as these, early village sites were busy places.

Use of products from trees goes well beyond those items we've noted above. The book titled *The 2003 Forests of Michigan* lists some 50 species of Michigan trees from which Native Americans derived a vast variety of uses and products. They included medicines and tonics, dyes, utensils, fuel, implements and weapons. Plants were a similar source of useful materials, and they were well acquainted with the identification and applications of all growing things.

Native Americans along the Looking Glass were blessed with abundant rich soils in the lands near the river. In fact, in Michigan, farming was their principal source of sustenance. A Michigan State University publication titled "Native Americans in the Great Lakes Region" tells us that around their villages they grew "corn, beans, peas, squash, and pumpkins," as well as "turnips, cabbage, parsnips, sweet potatoes, yams, and leeks." Of these, corn was the staple. Other sources mention sunflowers and tobacco. From the wilds they gathered "nuts, berries, wild plums, wild cherries, and pawpaws." In late summer, "wild rice was gathered around the Great Lakes" by canoe, from sluggish streams and shallow lakes. It was nutritious and easily stored for long periods.

The publication goes on to tell us that "Beaver, muskrat, racoon, deer, elk, bison and black bear were taken for the meat and hides." Such hides were utilized for both clothing and shelter. From the sugar maples which were, and still are, abundant in the more upland areas of the Looking Glass watershed, "sugaring" was a major activity in the early spring of each year, as the nights remained cool, but the days began to warm. Maple syrup and sugar were highly favored for energy and to sweeten foods, and used in abundance. Of course, they also ate many fish from the river. They even planted orchards of plums and apples.

It wasn't until near the mid-seventeenth century that the first Europeans made contact with Native Americans in Michigan. Thereafter, the French trappers, traders, explorers and missionaries had modest contact. Yet up through the early 1800s, the Chippewa/Ojibwa of the Looking Glass, as well as other of southern Michigan's Native Americans were largely unbothered by Whites. Not until statehood and the arrival of early settlers was there any real change. Until then, the Natives had lived peacefully in camps and villages along the Looking Glass for generations. The first settlers described them as peaceful, honest, hospitable, helpful, virtuous and guileless.

The *Michigan Pioneer and Historical Collections*, in one of its many volumes, indicates that "The Indians traded furs, berries and maple sugar for dry and fancy goods, ammunition and whiskey." There was such competition for furs in the early years that local traders would go out to the Indians' winter camps so as to beat out their competitors, often traveling from the post at Grand Rapids for long distances, including to the Looking Glass. Maple sugar also became a valuable article of trade, some even destined for merchants in Boston and New York. Some, reportedly, was transported as far away as Mexico! As recorded in an early journal, "During the spring, the Grand River (where the principal trading post was reached) was alive with canoes bringing sugar."

As the settlers increased, some Indians took on jobs with them to earn income. Others served as guides to the lands with which they were so familiar. They continued to trade venison and fish with the first settlers, offered items of clothing and sometimes even helped them clear the land and build cabins.

While there was some intermixing of the cultures for several decades afterward, eventually the Native Americans became increasingly assimilated into European lifestyles. As is evident today, little remains to identify the specific sites once regularly occupied along this river's banks. Most of them melted away after the 1830s, albeit for a very long time their earlier occupants were victims of ill-kept treaties and onerous reservation systems. They had ardently pursued their treaty rights through persistence and eloquent testimony. Lacking a written language, their speeches, and those of other Native Americans, were often very wise, flowery, moving and heart-felt, perhaps a trait developed over many centuries of verbal conveyance of memories and stories, interactions with early traders and settlers, and in treaty negotiations. ◀

❋ THE DEWITT VICINITY ❋

THE INTERURBAN CROSSING

▶ Not long after leaving Indian Green, we spotted from the river the rustic walking bridge associated with one of DeWitt's city parks. At the same time, along the south bank there is a tiny bayou, the outlet of Prairie Creek. It is not very conspicuous, but was once the source of power for an early sawmill and gristmill which we will discuss shortly. Far more obvious just beyond the rustic bridge, is a huge linear earth-fill with a flat top. It is most noticeable on the left side. DeWitt never enjoyed the advantage of being on a railroad, the boon of so many other settlements. But this is the point at which the Lansing and Suburban Electric Railway, the "Interurban," once crossed. Right here stood an imposing wooden trestle well above the Looking Glass. The tracks were completed in 1901, and while the final electrical components were being worked out, a steam locomotive and car were allowed to begin hauling passengers. As 1902 was coming to an end, so did that special permission, and electric passenger service became operational just a few months later.

Its northern terminus was St. Johns. Heading south it made several country stops, including "Merle Beach" (near Muskrat Lake at the corner of Jason and DeWitt Roads), "Bum's Corners" (at Alward Lake, a popular swimming destination near Loomis and Alward Roads), DeWitt village, "Dunhams" (on Herbison Road, west of Turner Road), and "Moots" (on Clark Road, a half mile west of Old 27). There were other stops as it continued south via Turner Street, pausing in North Lansing and then on to Lansing and East Michigan Avenue near the River. From Lansing, other routes also headed to Owosso and Flint, and a second south to Jackson and beyond. It was a very popular and active means of transportation until finally superseded by private autos and bus service. Its last car traveled the line in May of 1929. ◄

RIVER-PARKS AND MODERN ACCESS

It was in this area that we noted the first genuine ripples in the river, as it narrowed and the river picked up a little speed. The right bank was steep and high, the highest we had yet encountered on our journey. Nearby are the three contiguous riverside parks operated by the City of DeWitt, all on the left, making this a very pleasant area. Just before the Interurban was "River Trail Park." We had just passed under its rust-colored footbridge. It offers a pavilion, picnic tables, grills, play structures, and a modern restroom. There is no formal take-out spot. A short, paved river walk joins this and "Riverside Park," just past the Interurban. In addition to two small river observation decks, there is another playground here and modern toilets, as well as pavilion, picnic tables and grills. It also includes a modern canoe/kayak launch, which we used to exit. It consists of gleaming aluminum with a ramp on which the boater pulls himself up to exit the stream. The opposite end allows the boater to slide back down into the stream. You may recall our cautious entry of the kayaks back at the beginning of our journey. With this modern device, the boater need not stand up until safely exited of the water, or ready to slide back into the water. It is a wonderful and safer system compared to standing on the stream bank. The only drawback in this case is that the launch is located in a spot somewhat difficult to maneuver into from upriver. Also, the launch is a fair hike from the nearest parking lot, where your craft would need to be loaded or unloaded.

When you decide to move on, you will next pass under the bridge of – you guessed it - Bridge Street. You will note ornamental black railings supported by red-brick posts. Petunias, begonias and sweet potato vine were planted in bridge boxes by the DeWitt Millennium Garden Club, and are watered by City of DeWitt. Just beyond is where "Memorial Park" is located. Again, there is no take-out, and only a few facilities, but a nice riverside atmosphere.

THE SETTLING OF DEWITT

► **We took a brief rest here at the park, and as we do, I'll tell you about the interesting origin of the DeWitt area. The first white settler to build a home on the Looking Glass River was Captain David**

Scott, a soldier in the War of 1812. He arrived in the year 1833, having followed the old Indian trail later known as the Pontiac and Grand River Trail. We are again reminded of the difficulty of such a trip in those days. The *1880 History of Shiawassee and Clinton Counties* provides this account of their journey:

> *They began their pilgrimage in wagons drawn by ox-teams and laden with their household goods, their objective point being the land he entered* (purchased) *in Clinton County, embracing altogether 1,426 acres in various portions of the township. They forded rivers, drove into lakes, were frequently mired in dismal marshes, and pitched their tents where night overtook them, until their arrival ... Capt. Scott obtained the consent of the Indians* (at nearby Indian Green) *to occupy one of their wigwams for several weeks,* (until) *their own cabin was completed ... This Indian house was constructed of bark, with bunks on the side and a fire was built in the centre, the smoke of which escaped through a hole or remained in the room.*

Their first real home was a log cabin some 20-25 feet square, and located in what would become the middle of the block lying south and west of the intersection of future DeWitt's Main and Bridge Streets. For a short time their family was totally alone in the entire county, save for Scott's hired companion and George Campau's staff, who had established an Indian trading post at Maple Rapids to the north, just one year before. Unless...we were to also count the 17 head of cattle and one horse brought along by the Scott's. This being October, with no feed put up for the winter, natural grasslands and felled trees formed their sustenance that first winter. At one time these cattle strayed away and were gone for several days. When found, they were grazing on the distant ground now occupied by the State capitol building in Lansing.

Ground was broken for wheat the next summer. But milling it was no easy matter in those first years. He reported that the grain had to be:

> *hauled to Pontiac to be manufactured into flour. The trip to Pontiac with ox teams took about ten days...*(and)*...we had to camp out nights. We put the bells on the oxen and let them feed,*

but kept a good lookout for them, or we might be short a team in the morning.

Almost immediately, however, a flood of additional settlers descended upon the area. Scott added rooms to his home-site to take advantage of the accompanying need for temporary lodging. Also prompted and enticed by the growing influx, other entrepreneurs appeared to get a jump on Scott, and quickly platted three separate villages nearby.

Scott held the land of present-day DeWitt's downtown as a part of the large acreage he had originally purchased. The others were limited to less desirable sites, but were undaunted in their efforts. The first of these was initiated in the same year as Scott took up residence. <u>New Albany</u> was to be situated on the south side of the river. <u>Middletown</u> was platted in 1836 just east of present DeWitt, on both sides of the river, at the point where it is joined by Prairie Creek. <u>Old DeWitt</u> was laid out in 1837 east of and adjoining New Albany. Perhaps they had all been a bit too hasty. Perhaps most of the pioneers were still looking for farms, not city lots or to set up businesses. Middletown and Old DeWitt collapsed rather quickly, failing to attract a sufficient number of buyers, in spite of sale prices which had dropped to only one dollar per building lot. Both were defunct for failure to pay taxes by 1842.

<u>New Albany</u> fared somewhat better, and was a strong competitor, at least for a short time.

In New Albany there was also a store and a large hotel. While many lots were sold, many more were not, and those unsold were lost as tax delinquent between 1840 and 1848. A sawmill had been built in 1837, and a gristmill added in 1844, deriving its power from Prairie Creek. An historic marker, erected on the southeast corner of Locust and Dill (previously Mill) Streets provides this history:

> *Site of the first grist mill in Clinton County. Built in 1844 by Jesse and Milo Turner. Dam for water power was located one-half mile south on Prairie Creek. The head race was located in the nearby locust grove. The mill was destroyed by fire in 1901.*

It was Hiram Wilcox who in 1837 built that first sawmill in the county. It was placed into operation the following year. Its original water wheel was sixteen feet in diameter! We know that it was located southerly of the river and was water-powered. Its exact location has not been verified, although some have speculated that it was not far from the later gristmill which straddled the mill race (channel).

The site of the dam on Prairie Creek was located in what is now the valley of the Prairie Creek Golf Course. The water backed up by this dam shows clearly on an 1873 map of the area, and reached all the way south to Herbison Road. The mapmaker interestingly shows two "lines" running down from the dam, each apparently denoting a separate flow of water. One is rather winding, suggesting it is probably the original course of the creek. The other is straighter and more direct, and could very likely represent the very long separate mill race that had been built. Words entered by the mapmaker also seem to spell "S. Mill" down on the south bank of the Looking Glass, along the same "race" that served the grist mill, and thus placing both the saw mill and grist mill not far from the river.

Prior to the opening of the Turner gristmill, the local farmers had to go to the Wacousta mill, built in 1837, a distance of some eight difficult miles. For a time, New Albany also had a cooper's shop, blacksmith and a brewery. Some of these businesses had no counterpart across the river at the time. But eventually, DeWitt's community got the upper hand, and while some of the New Albany facilities operated for a while, others slowly disappeared.

In 1839, back at the site of present <u>DeWitt</u>, Scott had built a frame building for a store-room and grocery in 1839, located at the southeast corner of Bridge and Washington. It appears that it also served as a lodging facility, and was known as "Scott's." The rapidly growing settlement was declared by the legislature to serve as the county seat around 1840, a great boost for the area's prosperity. Then, in late 1841, perhaps noting the impending demise of the "original" (old) DeWitt, Captain Scott made his own move, platting out the village of (new) DeWitt in October, on the upland area on the north side of the river. In 1842 he followed up by building a very spacious and elegant hotel known as the "Clinton House" ("the big house") on the southwest corner of Bridge and Main. (It would be destroyed by fire in 1930). Several other entrepreneurs added their own businesses up on the hill. DeWitt boasted the first newspaper in the county, *The Clintonian*, in 1842. There was even a jail built there as early as 1843.

Scott's plat was destined to achieve far greater and lasting success than the others, bolstered initially by a number of factors. Foremost, perhaps, was its location right on the road considered the principal thoroughfare through this portion of the state, and thus followed by settlers. Added to this were the lovely location, the presence of Scott's hotel (which early on was heavily used by both passing settlers and as a local gathering spot), and the fact that for many decades it was the only settlement of size in the entire area. But likely also, there was Capt. Scott's known powers of persuasion and charm, his generosity, hospitality, and public spirit. Across the river in New Albany, a number of these industries also aided its prominence in a supportive way. Before long, DeWitt boasted a hotel, two general stores, a drug store, two millinery shops, a shoe store, a wagon shop, three blacksmith shops, a flour mill, two churches, professional offices and two sawmills. In addition to the mill on Prairie Creek, the other of those early sawmills appears to have been located behind the house of David Scott's son, built in 1861, and still located at 609 W. Main. An historic marker can be found there.

I found nothing more relating to the Scott mill, but a small stream did run the fill length of this piece of David Scott's property, all the way down to the river. In carefully scrutinizing an 1864 map of local landowners, I did find a couple of clues supporting the possibility of a mill. My examination appeared to show a small pond up on that stream which might have been the backwaters of a dam for a mill. Additionally, that map had some markings which may have indicated a short diversion of the Looking Glass itself, along its north side. Maybe, just maybe, this was the site of a mill race. Unfortunately, on these very early maps it is often difficult to discern the handwritten entries, so I cannot really confirm its location.

Upon Capt. Scott's death in 1851, his frame structure at Bridge and Washington passed into other hands, who added on and called it the "DeWitt House." But by the early 1900s Scott's was in a state of deterioration. In 1908 Peter Halterman built a house on that corner as a northern extension of the old building, which was known as "The Bee Hive." The original building has been since removed, but the addition remains to this day, occupied by the Chambers Chiropractic office, with an historical marker denoting the spot.

The settlement served as the county seat until 1857 when, favored by a new railroad through the town, it was moved to St. Johns. This proved a substantial setback, as many merchants and professionals then transferred their attention and presence to St Johns. Thereafter for a time, development in DeWitt's residential areas was particularly lagging. Yet it managed to survive, aided greatly by the prosperity of area farms still using the settlement for their needs. By the first years of the 1900s, it began to significantly thrive once again through the persistence, strong leadership, dedicated businesses, and committed citizens who found it a most desirable place to live and do business. It was incorporated as a <u>village</u> in about 1928, and a <u>city</u> in 1965. It continues to thrive today, and offers numerous places of refreshment with just a short walk up the hill from the take-out park. ◄

Before proceeding with our story, I want to point out that my own work of researching the DeWitt vicinity's rich history was independently gathered mostly from a variety of the earliest sources available, and includes just the essential early highlights. But I certainly want to draw your attention to the far more detailed account by Kenneth Coin in his book *DeWitt Area History*. It makes great reading, and covers just about everything you would ever want to know about the local area.

✳ THE NAMINGS: ✳ DEWITT, CLINTON AND THE LOOKING GLASS

One last thing before we slide our kayaks back into the water and depart DeWitt. You may be wondering, as I did: How did the city and county get the names DeWitt and Clinton? How did the Looking Glass River get its name?

DEWITT AND CLINTON

It was rather common practice in the days of new settlements in new lands, to name them after places which the pioneers had left behind, perhaps another country or another state, or a more recent hometown, as is the case with "New" Albany. Another favorite was to name them for prominent citizens or politicians of past or present. It is really not so surprising, then, that DeWitt and Clinton were applied to this geographic area. In fact, many other Midwestern states also adopted either DeWitt or Clinton or both as their county, township or village names. Here's why.

▶ DeWitt Clinton was a man born in 1769 of a famous military father, James Clinton, who had been a Brigadier General in the Revolutionary Army in 1776. But DeWitt followed a different track. He was elected to the state legislature of New York in 1798, and as the mayor of New York City in 1803. He was a presidential candidate in 1812, and governor of New York state in 1817. It was as governor that he envisioned a project which would make him most remembered. As a resident of New York, and an influential statesman, he was aware of the great influx of immigrants moving from the harbors of New York, looking to establish farms of their own to the west. But travel was difficult across the terrain of New York. As a substantial aid, and under his oversight, the Erie Canal was initiated. It was completed in 1825, providing a direct and continuous water route across New York to Buffalo on Lake Erie. Many of the Michigan-bound pioneers made use of this canal.

Having visited some of the sites where the long-defunct canal once passed, I can testify to the precise engineering and intense labor that were required to construct these waterways. There might be long expanses dug deeply through ordinary fields. But more often than not, the route would obviously follow the valleys of <u>existing</u> rivers and streams. Most had to be deepened, and in other places concrete barriers were built on each side to contain and deepen the waters. Because of the constantly changing elevations, locks were necessary at intervals to lift or lower the barges to the next level.

These barges, on which were loaded the homesteaders and their property, were towed by rope along the dug canal or enhanced natural waterways by horses or mules walking along the bank. An early traveler from New York, John Nowlin, relates:

> *We embarked on a canal boat and moved slowly night and day ... Sometimes when we came to a lock, father got off and walked a mile or two ... when we came to a favorable place, father signaled to the steersman, and he turned the boat up. Father jumped on to the side of the boat.*

Another traveler, John F. Hinman, who settled in DeWitt township, and whose family name would rest on a local road which we would later pass under in our own journey, gives this more detailed account of his 1838 journey by canal boat:

I left Utica (New York) *about 4 o'clock P.M., on the canal...the baggage having been placed on the forward deck...and covered up with a large canvas covering ... Little tables were placed in the center of the cabin ... At about six o'clock ... all the passengers* (there were about 30) *sat down to tea, coffee, bread, butter, liver, steak, potatoes, pickles, ham and sausage ... At 8 o'clock* (A. M., we were served the same meal) *all over again ... The dinner was a duplicate of the breakfast ... After the supper was over the men nearly all went on deck.* (It was necessary) *to duck one's head every five minutes, whenever the man at the helm called out "bridge;" and ...when the cry was "low bridge," to get down nearly flat ...* (At bedtime, I) *found suspended on either side of the cabin, three long tiers of hanging sacks, and on each sack a small sheet, pillow and blanket ... We arrived in Rochester Sunday morning, the 10th...as the boats did not run on that day ...* (Two days later we arrived at Buffalo, and) *took passage for Detroit on board the steamer.*

Once reaching Lake Erie, the homesteaders could embark on schooners or steamships to Michigan, most often the port of Detroit. From there they would transition to horse- and ox-drawn wagons to complete their trip inland. Many of Michigan's early homesteaders arrived via the Erie Canal, so surely it helped influence the selection of "Clinton" as the county name, and "DeWitt" as the local village. The county of Clinton was named by the Territorial legislature as early as 1831. The township was so noted in 1836, and the village in 1841. ◄

LOOKING GLASS

As we had thus far drifted peacefully and effortlessly down this wide stretch of river, smooth and ripple-less, providing perfect reflections of overhanging trees, it was easy to see how it got its English name – the Looking Glass. Author Doc Fletcher pointed out in his book, *Michigan Rivers Less Paddled*, that the famous Robert Louis Stevenson contemplated this phenomenon in his poem "Looking-Glass River," published in 1885 along with other poems in the collection, *Child's Garden of Verses*:

Smooth it slides upon its travel,
Here a wimple, there a gleam –
O the clean gravel!
O the smooth stream!

Sailing blossoms, silver fishes,
Pave pools as clear as air –
How a child wishes
To live down there!

We can see our colored faces
Floating on the shaken pool
Down in cool places,
Dim and very cool.

A paddling contributor to the paddling.com website recently wrote of his experience:

All in all, I love paddling this river because of the laziness of the current and the beauty and seclusion of the surroundings, and

The paddling is easy as the current is at times unnoticeable unless a leaf is floating along on the surface.

▶ **So the concept is readily understood. But when was this name first applied to our own river? The atlases of Clinton and surrounding counties, published in the 1870's, use the name "Looking Glass" on their maps. An 1864 map of Eagle Township also applies the name. It is shown even earlier on the 1830s plat of Middletown, near DeWitt village. If it was already named when the very first settler arrived on the river in 1833, then who had applied it? There were additional sources to check.**

As we've previously pointed out, in order for would-be settlers to locate a piece of property and claim it for purchase, a thorough survey of such sections of the state was first necessary. These surveyors preceded any settlers, and I was curious as to whether they had found a river name associated with their initial entry upon the land. As the surveyor of Shiawassee reached the river in 1823, he on several crossings called it simply the "stream," or the "river." However, on other occasions, he specifically called it the "Looking

Glass." The surveyors of Clinton County in 1826, and of Ionia County in 1826 and 1827 both referred clearly to the "Looking Glass."

So if it wasn't the earliest settlers, nor even the earlier surveyors who named the river, then who was it? Who was here before that? The answer would be the early French explorers, trappers, traders and Jesuit priests, who had been making excursions into the interior of the entire Great Lakes region and future Michigan territory since the 1600's, making periodic use of the area's renowned waterways. French traders often set up their posts along the Grand River, as far east as Ionia and even beyond. Obviously, they had made their entrance to the interior from the west, from Lake Michigan, and traveled upstream on the Grand.

In the other direction, the most prominent and earliest of the French settlements would be Detroit, itself a French word meaning "the straits." Well-known also is the French origin of the Grand River, the longest in the state, which they appropriately dubbed "le Riviere Grand." The Michigan Territory surveyor who traversed Ionia County in 1826 added to his notes after crossing a small stream which emptied into the Maple River just above Muir village, that the French had named it "la Riviere Aux Rochers." That is the River of Rocks, or today's "Stoney Creek." The Maple itself they called "la Riviere DuPlain," the River of the Plains. In the case of the Flint River, it is clear that the French used the same terminology as the local Indians had already applied to the river. The Natives called it Peiconigowink, literally "River of the Fire Stone." The French translated this to their equivalent "Riviere de la Pierre." The English translation was simply, the "Flint." But so far, nothing about a French reference to the Looking Glass.

Pursuing the French angle a little further, I visited the Michigan State University library's map room, where staff helped me to locate a copy of the 1744 "Carte Des Lacs Du Canada," or map of the lakes of Canada (Great Lakes Region). All information was of course in French, including *all* of the major rivers flowing into Lake Michigan from around the state's still distorted exterior. Unfortunately, the lesser interior rivers, perhaps not yet so rigorously explored, were omitted. Maybe it never was given a French title.

So I needed to look even earlier in time, to the indigenous peoples. Somehow, I would need to determine the meaning of the "original" term applied by the Native Americans. Earliest records indicate that the local Natives called it "Wabwaysin," or perhaps

"Wahwasin." In seeking after its original Native meaning, I spent a couple hours among the fine resources available in the library of Michigan State University, but to no avail. Upon departing, Bonnie and I decided to drive over to the Nokomis Learning Center in Okemos, which is "a Native American cultural learning center...dedicated to the preservation and presentation of Anishinaabe culture." As good fortune would have it, that very night a specialist in the Ojibwa language was scheduled to teach a class there on the subject. My question was presented, and I received a very thrilling report.

Alphonse Pitawanakwat has made a concerted effort to study, apply and preserve the native Anishinaabe/Ojibwa language originally spoken in the area. He had once served as a lecturer of the Ojibwa language at the University of Michigan, and now teaches young Natives and others the fine points of the language, helping to keep that core part of the culture alive and well. He believes that the more proper rendering of the old term for this river should be

"Waabawidsan"

And its meaning, when translated into English is to...:

"Look-at-yourself", or *"See-yourself"*

Consequently, today's name for the Looking Glass River is, in fact, a proper reproduction of its original Native description, the "see-yourself-river!"

As you will see later under the discussion of "Wacousta," another source has suggested a river name stemming from another Indian word. While that is less likely, we will chat more about that a little later. ◄

✳ ON THE RIVER – TRIP FOUR ✳
(DeWitt to Airport)

We settled back into these reflecting waters with our kayaks, and not yet far from DeWitt, recalled from a prior float through this section that here we had surprised two deer watching us intently from a woodsy area on the left bank. We had been able to approach within just a few kayak-lengths before they concluded we had invaded their "space" and decided to mosey on.

A rather significant log jam now faced us just a little farther on. Log jams are formed when a single large fallen tree or limb blocks much or all of the river. Subsequent floating debris from upstream then also catches against the larger tree, creating an impassable "jam." These can be extremely dangerous, as canoes and kayaks are easily overturned when their forward progress is stalled, yet the continuing force of the current pushes at the bottom of the craft and overturns it, tossing the occupant into the jam as well. Take out in advance or near shore, to pull your craft around the jam. Or, as we found out at this site, the "Friends" had already been busy and had cut through a small channel along the left edge. We would see lots more evidence of their helpfulness along our route.

MCGUIRE PARK

Just a little farther downstream, though not very evident from the water, is "McGuire Park." As we approached, a distinct hill topped by Lake Geneva homes moved in from the left, and an observation deck on the right marked the park's location. Accessed from West Main Street, it offers a small playground, short paved walking trail, two pavilions, picnic tables, grill, basketball court and modern toilets. It is also the site of the city fire department. There is no formal take-out, but the bank is usually adequate. Recall that this was probably also the site of an early Native American garden.

LAKE GENEVA

As quickly as it appeared, the hill on our left subsided into a little valley. A small stream flows out of that valley and into a small bayou connected to the river. Just a short way up that stream is an earthen dam with small culverts protruding. Lake Geneva is now very close by, just out of sight.

▶ In relatively recent times DeWitt was rapidly continuing its expansion into nearby lands. As late as 1960, this area less than one mile southwest of the current town center was still farmland. In its midst was a large marshy depression. This valley drained what little standing water there was slowly down to the Looking Glass nearby. That was all about to change dramatically. Kenneth Coin, author of the book *DeWitt Area History*, provides this fine summary of events:

> *In 1961, real estate broker and developer, Don Foote of Lansing, revealed plans for the development of a 300-acre housing project southwest of the village of DeWitt. The Lake Geneva Development Company of which Foote was president had acquired the farm and marshland from five neighboring farms.*
>
> *The marsh situated on the land had for decades been a favored hunting and huckleberry picking area. It was cleared of its trees and brush in 1961 and at the northern end an earthen dam was built. Water from the Looking Glass River was then pumped into the 62-acre hole thus forming a lake with an average depth of 14 feet…The Lake Geneva area was annexed into the city of DeWitt in 1967.*

The 125-foot long dam was of earthen construction, with an outlet into the prior natural valley and thence into the Looking Glass. The original source of pumping was the small bayou just to our left. In time the river ceased to be the source of water for maintaining the water levels in Lake Geneva. Instead, two large wells were drilled adjacent to the lake, and pumping is now required every summer to sustain the water level. The surface of the new lake is now perched about 15-20 feet above the river. ◀

IS IT SCHAVEY OR SCHOEWE?

Schavey Road will be coming up soon, forewarned by the fact that Howe Road is running close by and parallel to the river. Schavey Road Bridge is another flat concrete structure. The lower rail is of concrete, framing little concrete "windows." It is topped with an upper rail of metal tubing.

► In 1835 Franklin Oliver, his wife and two or three children arrived in the area from New York. They purchased and settled here in Section 7, including both the east and west sides of present Schavey Road, and north of Herbison. Obviously, as we will see, it also included this Looking Glass River frontage. He was quickly involved in local affairs. In 1840 he was active in forming a church to be in fellowship with the Baptist Brethren of DeWitt. In 1841 he was elected as the fourth supervisor of DeWitt Township. He established a burial ground on his homestead and in 1843 deeded it to the township. In an effort of consolidation, these graves were soon removed to the location of the present DeWitt cemetery on North Bridge Street.

Author Kenneth Coin adds from his 1983 book, *DeWitt Area History*:

> *In 1839 he constructed a saw mill on the Looking Glass River near his cabin. This mill could never be operated properly and was not used to any extent. ...Traces of Oliver's mill are still visible on the south bank of the river, even after a lapse of over one hundred and forty years.*

This description would place it somewhere within the mile downstream of the Lake Geneva outlet. But I was unable to spot anything from the water, even after returning some time later with my grandson, Carter, to look for signs. Perhaps it was simply tucked away in the underbrush, and I missed it.

In about 1883, according to a recent article in the *DeWitt-Bath Review*, some 166 acres of the property was purchased by the Theodore Schoewe family. Yes, "Schoewe!" And the name attached to the road became "Schavey," the name we see today. Perhaps this should come as no big surprise, as the native pronunciation of the German name "Schoewe" would sound very much like "Schavey." Unfortunately, this kind of shift from misspellings occurred often in olden times.

With a lucky glimpse, you can see the brick farmhouse they built on your left, just before passing under the bridge. The barn sat just across the road. They planted corn and other crops. After changing hands several more times in the ensuing years, and then standing vacant, it was acquired by the Sisters of Mercy in the 1970's. They have since restored it, and continue to maintain it in attractive condition. ◄

Along the stretch of river from here at Schavey Road and down to Airport Road, several ponds have been dug in the nearby lowlands. The first of them are just over the left bank, and then a few more over the right bank. While not visible from the river, you will be able to notice a number of homes built around them as part of several subdivisions.

ABOUT THE WATER

Also along this stretch, large isolated boulders are becoming more frequent. As you keep an eye out for them, glimpse below you into the water and note that throughout our journey this water which has been supporting and moving our kayaks generally runs fairly clear. Most often we can at least faintly see the bottom. But after all, water is simply "water," right? Actually, the nature of river water can be quite variable. Some characteristics are of natural origin. For example, a spring-fed northern stream on a gravelly streambed may be particularly cold and clear. A sluggish southern Michigan stream though clay soils may be cloudy and warm. The Tahquamenon River in the eastern Upper Peninsula has a distinctive reddish-brown color, stained by the tannins of the many trees growing in the swamps through which it flows.

There are also characteristics which are not evident to the naked eye, and they may be even more important to the quality of the water in the river. Since we will soon be reaching the outlet of a major sewage treatment facility for the region, it will be timely to review three particular features of significance.

Water Levels

Most of us would not be aware that the river levels of today are notably lower than in the days of the Native Americans and early settlers. Shortly we will tell of boats and rafts plying the Looking Glass farther downstream. Looking at the river depth today, it appears unlikely that such would have been possible unless there was a greater flow of water.

Especially in late season, some sections will now barely float a canoe. At an earlier time, the light Indian canoes could negotiate much of the river's length. An 1840 report indicates that in those days the Looking Glass could be "ascended by canoes almost to its source." We have already found that such is impossible in much of the upper reaches today. A number of factors have contributed to a shallower and more irregular flow in modern times. A writer in the *Archaeological Atlas of Michigan* records that "the water-table of the southern part of the state ... has been lowered four or five feet by clearing the land and by the numerous ditches that have been dug for draining the low and swampy places." While water table reduction does not translate directly to an equivalent drop in river levels, it was nonetheless a contributing influence.

Storm Water

It is important to note that river water is very susceptible to the influences of man. We have already discussed the impacts of county drains and lost floodplains. But there is much more. Where developments such as cities and parking lots are constructed near rivers, storm water discharge pipes can often be seen emptying water directly into the river. They lead from culverts, ditches, catch basins or other open waterways which collect excessive storm water runoff, and whisk it away from streets, parking lots, and residential/business areas where damaging temporary flooding might otherwise occur. Such waters are carried directly to local natural streams and rivers, in this case the Looking Glass. That's the good news.

The bad news is that it also carries away any other materials which might be swept along by the runoff – anything that might have been accidentally, intentionally, or carelessly, dropped or deposited in such areas. This might include dirt, melting salt, rubber tire fragments, gas and oil drippings, paints and soaps, household products, grass clippings, autumn leaves, cigarette butts, fast food wrappings and other litter. It often also includes less obvious runoff inclusions such as lawn and farm fertilizers, animal waste, pesticides and herbicides, eroded soil, and chemical pollutants. Many of the items often seen caught in swirling river eddies derive from such sources.

Not only do these spoil the river's beauty, they also affect water quality. Suspended soil particles cloud streams, blocking sunlight that supports healthy plant growth. Soil also settles onto river bottoms, covering the gravel beds that many fish and aquatic insects use to reproduce. Various nutrients, as from lawn and farm fertilizer, can over-stimulate growth of undesirable weeds and algae, blocking sunlight and consuming oxygen. Direct disposal of grass clippings and leaves has similar effects. Other chemicals simply and directly pollute the waters.

In response to these potentially harmful effects from "polluted" storm water runoff, the industry is already looking at additional safeguards, both in construction techniques and possible treatments, to help assure that even these effects are mitigated.

Clean Water Facilities

The river makes a slight bend to the right, and then runs fairly straight for a short distance. Along this stretch take note of a house on the left bank with a nicely manicured two-level lawn. A couple canoes are hung on racks near an observation deck. By pure coincidence, this happens to be the house of Larry Arbanas, river enthusiast and a charter member of the "Friends of the Looking Glass." About here you will begin to hear the sound of rushing water. The source is found just downstream.

▶ **But first we will make note of one more historic feature. Notice the very small stream slipping out of the marshy lowland on the right. Records indicate that "there are the remains of a mill at the foot of a drain which probably was a small stream at one time." This would appear to be the present Faiver Drain, which now extends north nearly to Cutler Road. Just a stone's throw downstream of its juncture here with the Looking Glass, I did find two small concrete structures visible only when the vegetation is low in the spring. I wondered if they may have been the sawmill footings? Or, given the low swampland abundant here, might the dam have been built just a bit farther up the incoming stream, where the banks were higher? Before moving on, take a look just once more slightly up the Faiver Drain. On its left bank are the remains of a canoe rack which would have held multiple canoes. I was told by a nearby resident that there was once a livery operating from this location.**

Back on the Looking Glass, and just beyond this, on both banks and extending to the river's edge, are raised man-made earthworks. The ends of the grade on both sides were faced with carefully laid stone-work. Long ago, Herbison Road did not make the southerly bend to avoid the river as it now does. Rather it ran straight west, crossing the Looking Glass at this point and continuing on to connect with Airport Road. Sometime, perhaps around 1940, a milk truck was crossing here and collapsed the bridge. It was not rebuilt, and the road was re-routed. ◀

*****

We now need to keep an eye out for the rushing water that we already heard from some distance back. It shows up on our left; a large concrete-encased pipe is emptying water into the river. Technically, it is called an "outfall pipe." Were we to follow it backwards to its source, we would find that this one originates at a wastewater treatment plant located just across Herbison Road. It is a "Clean Water Facility," overseen by the Southern Clinton County Municipal Utilities Authority, and operated cooperatively by the City of DeWitt and portions of three neighboring townships. Having just passed with our kayaks through the city and several subdivisions, along with its concentrated human populations and activities, it is obvious that some provision must be made for sanitary sewers.

Several other treatment facilities and sewage lagoons farther upstream clean and return some water to the watershed. They serve the cities of Perry and Laingsburg, as well as the mobile home parks at Countryside Village and Capitol Crossings. However, the largest and most fully developed is this DeWitt-area facility, located on the south side of Herbison Road, about two miles downstream from the main intersections of DeWitt. The facility provides a means for safe and sanitary treatment and disposal of wastes collected from publicly-operated sanitary sewer systems. Systems like this prevent dangerous polluted waters from seeping down into the groundwater which serves our water wells, or reaching the river systems and polluting those waters. Clearly, we would not want any of this to reach our rivers and lakes, as was too often the case long ago.

▶ **Early in 1975 DeWitt Township and the City of DeWitt were notified by the Michigan Water Resources Commission that their then wastewater plant discharges were no longer meeting water pollution control requirements. In fact, local residents recall public health advisories to the effect that they were not to drink or even come in contact with the river water. This dire situation resulted in the construction of a new facility to serve multiple jurisdictions. It went into operation in late 1980.** ◀

The facility works like this. The sewer system is an elaborate network of over 200 miles of sewer collection pipes moving waste from the drains and sewers of homes, industry, schools and businesses. All of them eventually lead to this treatment facility, but they need a little help. It is not possible for gravity alone to do the job over all of the extensive serviced area. Hence some 50 lift sites, or pumping stations, at key locations pump the sewage to higher levels wherever necessary, allowing gravity to then move it ever closer to the facility. Here the waters are cleaned and purified, removing harmful bacteria, so they can be returned to the river. The cleansing methods used are physical, biological and chemical. Solids and larger sediments are settled or screened out. Most of these are treated and recycled as nutrients on farmland. The other remaining heavier materials are disposed of in landfills.

Materials which make it through the screens and settling tanks are subjected to biological actions by micro-organisms, which convert them to safer products. Some settle out, and some pass on to the final phase. There they go through fine filters of anthracite coal, sand and gravel. Finally, it is disinfected with chlorine. When ready for discharge, the purified water moves into an underground pipe beneath Herbison Road, and via a narrow underground easement between two houses to the outfall here at the riverside. This is a simplified explanation of a complex process, but shows how carefully those in charge handle the materials to assure that water re-entering the Looking Glass is pure.

And so, to summarize, unfiltered storm water drains might actually decrease the quality of the water of the looking Glass, due to our own careless deposits. On the other hand, treatment plant discharges are actually often cleaner than the river into which it is dumped. This is certainly a wonderful testament to the ingenuity of mankind, and particularly here, our caring local citizens.

Water Quality Tests

Just how does the Looking Glass rate overall as to its quality and purity? A survey report issued in 2008 by the Michigan Department of Environmental Quality was based on biological, chemical and physical habitat conditions which they had analyzed at numerous points along the Looking Glass and its feeder tributaries:

> *The entire Looking Glass watershed is designated as a warmwater stream ... Land use is dominated by agriculture (47%), followed by a mix of grass/pasture area (21%), forest (18%), water (10%), residential (3%) and commercial and industrial (1%) ... Stations sampled ... had habitat ratings from poor to excellent, and macroinvertebrate ratings ranged from acceptable to excellent.*

Average ratings give a better picture than the ranges. Habitat evaluations were "good" at at least 50% of the test stations, and "marginal" at the rest, with the exception of just one which was rated as "poor." The state of the macroinvertebrate community was rated as within an "acceptable" range at every station, with the exception of one which was rated "excellent." It appears we can be very proud of our river, those who watch over it, and the citizens who collectively are careful with the resource.

Perpetuation of this condition cannot rely solely on today's citizens, however; the next generation must also be instilled with such love and concern. Fortunately, enterprising schoolteachers in the area are doing just that. Of note is Kari Roy, sixth-grade science teacher at DeWitt's Herbison Woods Elementary School. She is known for using the outdoors to help students learn, and involving them in community projects. Field trips include one to the water filtration plant. Her students are also raising young Chinook salmon for planting in the Looking Glass. This project expands to studies of life cycles, ecology and the environment, and invasive species.

Cammie Jones is a fourth-grade teacher at DeWitt's Scott Elementary School. Her focus is often on nature-based activities, seeking to "provide unique and memorable learning experiences." One of these is sampling and testing water from the Looking Glass. Her class also cooperates with MSU in macroinvertebrate studies on the river.

In recognition of their efforts and methods, both teachers have recently received the "Excellence in Education" award from the Michigan Lottery program.

With Many Thanks to the "Friends"

The river remains sensitive to our actions or inactions. It can be polluted, its beauty destroyed, its animal and plant communities placed in jeopardy, its fishes deprived of oxygen. Who will continue to protect it and watch over it? For one, each of us needs to demonstrate our concern. Innovative teachers, like those noted above, do their part. And fortunately, there is also an organization which recognizes this resource. While it promotes the river's appropriate recreational use, it also presents environmental cautions and information for managers, and remains on the lookout for problems. That organization is called the "Friends of the Looking Glass." Their stated goals include to:

- promote responsible land use and environmental practices within the watershed
- communicate watershed information to managers, decision makers, riparian landowners and the general public

- develop networks with stakeholders in the Looking Glass Watershed, and
- promote responsible recreational use of the Looking Glass River. Check them out at www.lookingglassriverfriends and review their informative river handbook.

It was 1990 when Gloria Miller, a retired school teacher, had begun to focus her environmental and recreational interests on local rivers. Having grown up just a half mile from the Looking Glass, it was only natural that it became one of her greatest interests. With other like-minded people, she formed the "Friends of the Looking Glass River" organization, and served many years as its president. One of their projects has been to organize and conduct an annual river log-jam cleanup. Without it, recreational canoeing and kayaking would soon become extremely difficult, if not impossible.

As with any organization, the challenge is to maintain public interest and volunteer commitment and input. There is turnover, and help is always needed. If you are one of those who treasures the beauty and values of the Looking Glass, please consider joining with them and helping out.

THE NILES AND GROGER EXPERIENCE

While we have had easy going since departing DeWitt, it was once quite a different matter. As we've already noted, the first settlers, including the families who followed Scott's lead to the DeWitt area, faced difficult travel trying to move heavily-laden wagons over the muddy trails. Such trails had long supported Native foot traffic. Early resident Alexander B. Copley records that since about the late 1700s, Native Americans had also been utilizing ponies for transporting trade goods, their own camp supplies, and of course, their own people. But they were wholly unfit for repeated wear by the pioneers with their stock and wagons, especially where they traversed the numerous marshlands and swamps. The stretch of river which we were now experiencing is testimony to the sometimes extraordinary efforts of pioneers to avoid or endure such hardships on the road.

▶ **In 1831, the New York families of Anthony Niles and Stephen Groger were among many others traveling with all their possessions aboard the steamship *Robert Fulton* from Buffalo across Lake Erie to Detroit. This route suggests the likely prior travel upon** the Erie Canal across parts of New York. Upon arrival in Detroit, two men with teams were hired to bring the families to Troy. The following year, Niles and two others went ahead to investigate the land to the westward, following the familiar Indian trail leading from Pontiac to the mouth of the Looking Glass. Having been favorably impressed with the lands they passed, they returned and set out again with their families in early 1834. At this point we will follow the record provided by our 1880 *History of Shiawassee and Clinton Counties*, occasionally edited by me for brevity and clarity:

> *In the township of DeWitt, the teams which had been secured to bring their families and goods were mired, the horses being 'all down at the same time.' The women, children, and goods were carried through the deep mud and water several rods to higher ground, the horses after much trouble were finally extricated, and by means of ropes the wagons were drawn across the marsh, and after an infinite number of trying and tedious delays the party reached the cabin of Capt. Scott ... While the families of Niles and Groger elected to continue on the land path behind a yoke of oxen, three of their traveling companions decided they had had quite enough of the muddy roads, and decided instead to build boats and a raft to assist in the expedition.*
>
> *After several days' diligent work, they completed two boats and a raft. The boats, commonly known as dugouts, were each made from a whitewood* log, and were about eighteen feet long and two and a half feet wide. They were lashed together, the goods were loaded on the raft, which was a huge, unmanageable concern, and the trip downstream commenced. After proceeding about six miles the raft struck a snag, and all efforts to free it proved futile. The party went ashore in the boats and camped to await the arrival of the Niles and Groger parties, who were trying to make their way through the wilderness, and who did not make their appearance along the shore until evening. The next morning, the water having risen somewhat during the night, the raft was freed, the families carried across the river in the boats, and the journey resumed.*
>
> *In the afternoon, a landing was made on the south shore of the river near what would be the present Eden Trail in Eagle Township, some 12-14 river miles from their put-in point at Capt. Scotts. The next morning the goods were transferred from*

the raft to the boats and the raft was abandoned. They then continued their way down the river, and finally reached the Indian village located at the present site of Portland. The Niles family spent two weeks there living in a wigwam, not unlike the Scott family had done back at the DeWitt site just a year before.

*(Whitewood is likely the tulip tree, sometimes also called yellow-poplar, which in these early days was often used by Native Americans to make dugout canoes, due to its light weight and easily-shaped wood.) ◄

As we here view the size of the Looking Glass, we can readily recall my earlier remark that in early days the Looking Glass carried a considerably higher volume of water than today, so that the rafting idea was not as ridiculous as it may now seem.

ABOUT BRIDGES

The earliest settlers were required to cross many streams and rivers as they traveled through southern Michigan. Without bridges, they searched for fords – shallow areas with sound bottoms, where a horse and wagon could simply be driven across. But the state legislature, and eventually local government units, soon recognized that both roads and bridges were essential to encouraging settlement. Slowly, work had begun on both.

At first, given the complexity and cost, bridges were few in number. Yet today, in the course of the full length of the river, culverts and bridges denote river crossings at least 50 times! In spite of this large number, there are still about ten sections of river where roads do not cross for two river miles, and a couple more where three-mile stretches are free of such crossings. These few sections remain particularly "on the wild side."

The 50 or so bridges which cross the Looking Glass seem to be of considerable variety. Some are very picturesque, while others are rather bland and stark. Unfortunately, in modern times the trend is toward the latter, as they are less expensive to build and maintain. Very few of the present-day bridges are truly historic. Within Michigan's "water wonderland" as a whole, more than 10,000 bridges cross streams. Of those, over 6,000 are located on county roads or city streets, and the remainder are on the state highway system. As we proceed, I will focus on a number of them.

*****

For a time after leaving the discharge of the Clean Water Facility, we passed by numerous homes built along the left bank of the river. They cease when the river corridor once again widens into marshland. At this point, on the left side and before the Airport Road, we reached DeWitt Township's "Looking Glass Riverfront Park." Here there is another modern canoe launch, being again handicap-accessible. There is parking off Herbison Road, but no toilets. The five-acre site, at the intersection with Blue Spruce Drive, also offers picnic tables, grills, and a river observation deck. Note that in high water it is not unusual for parts of this area to be under water. Here we removed our kayaks to wait for another day.

※ ON THE RIVER – TRIP FIVE ※
(Airport to Wacousta)

AIRPORT ROAD BRIDGE

Due to various obligations and activities, it was many weeks and mid-August before I was able to get back on the river. There were no high water problems now! During the interim, the weather had been hot and rainfall scarce. The river level had dropped dramatically. Bonnie was not able to accompany me on this trip. We had just returned from a week's vacation and she felt an obligation to tend to catch-up chores around the house and yard. I had similar chores awaiting, but was successful in ignoring them for a time.

Bonnie dropped me off, and it was 9:30 AM when I got underway. It was good to get on the river early. Not only was the air temperature cooler, but the sun was on my left, so that the trees on the left bank cast welcome shade on the river. A single delicate and flaming-red cardinal flower greeted me just across from the boat launch. They would become quite numerous from here on. There were some minor ripples as I approached the Airport Road bridge, a sure sign that water levels were lower. It would become increasingly evident during this trip that a canoe might have difficulty negotiating some sections late in the season.

The bridge is identified by a small white sign on its side. It is yet another flat concrete structure, with double squared-metal rails along the sides. As previously mentioned, it is believed that somewhere in this vicinity was also the site of some Indian Mounds. Much of the area near the river is marshy. The nearby uplands, including some modest hills, are now covered with several subdivisions. This makes it hard to visualize where such mounds might have been, but it certainly wouldn't have been impossible.

Beyond Airport Road, the river speed picks up just a bit. The bottom displays more cobblestone and gravel. This is of course a favorable sign for river quality and habitat for some fish species. A tiny stream, which has drained the wetlands just to the south, enters from the left. Farther down on the right I was somewhat surprised to see a few branches of a maple in bright red array. On the other hand, this is not uncommon in August when occasional individual trees are in particularly stressed situations – saturated soils or drying soils, insect and disease or other health problems. Later in the trip, when fall colors are becoming more common, I will have more to say about this color-changing process in trees.

As I paused to get a photo of this tree, a hawk flew overhead and on upriver, likely searching for its next meal. Several very fine homes were appearing on the right. A few insects were also making themselves known, perhaps not surprising for this time of year. A few areas of ripples continued to appear whenever the river was shallower and the bottom covered with fist-sized stones. A log-jam that the Friends had obviously worked on in higher water forced me to get out of my kayak to pull it over the now exposed lower limb of a fallen tree. A great blue heron launched itself, the first I'd seen in a while.

So far on today's trip, as with most of the upstream river, both banks of the river have tended to be low and associated with wetlands. Now, suddenly and straight ahead, was a high bank. It forced the river to the left and remained adjacent for some distance. On the nearby upland, if we could see them, were several very large ponds. This ridge has been the site of gravel excavations for some time. Several of them have already been abandoned and converted to housing subdivisions with the ponds as focal points. Others will likely soon follow.

Very soon another log jam appeared, which looked to span the entire river. But I found a small passage on the far right, allowing negotiation around a large boulder which also pokes up in the river at that point. After a rather long stretch of nothing but woods, a house appeared on the left as the river turned back to the right. The owner greeted me from the deck as I passed by, and inquired about my trip in the few moments before the current carried me by. There are lots of cobblestones here. I also spotted my very first bass, and it looked like a keeper.

Not long afterward a power line crossed the river. The route just ahead looked somewhat confusing, but just stay to the right for easy passage. As the river widened ahead, the largest tree I've seen so far on the entire journey – a silver maple – could be seen on the left. A hunter's tree stand was nearby. Three ducks were drifting on the river where a small stream entered from the right. The bugs, while not numerous, were becoming more annoying. I didn't want to slap my glasses into the river, as I had once done many years ago on the Fox River in the Upper Peninsula. So, I reluctantly got out the bug spray. This kept them away for the balance of the trip.

LOWELL ROAD BRIDGE

Continue to be alert for areas of large boulders. There were quite a few of them in this stretch.

Rounding a bend to the left, the very picturesque Lowell Road bridge came into view. Again, its name appears on the side of the bridge. The 91-foot iron bridge which had previously stood here at Lowell Road since its construction in 1896 was removed in more recent times. Until then it was one of the oldest remaining structures on the Looking Glass River. The HistoricBridges.org website described it as a "Metal 6 Panel Pin-Connected Pratt Through Truss, Fixed." Got that? Their further comments: "An odd, yet stunning, through truss that will no longer beautify Clinton County." Listed as "Dismantled," it was replaced in 2006 with this shiny new galvanized bridge of today. Thankfully, in keeping with this very country-ish setting, the new one has some character, with arms some 15 feet tall forming picturesque interlaced "V's." If you needed to take out here, the place would be on the right bank just before the bridge. Just keep in mind the uncertainty as to whether this is road right-of-way or private property. There is not any public parking.

If you are continuing on, as I did, be aware that there is a line of rocks piled fully across the river right under this bridge. Clearly they were placed there artificially. And we would encounter many more such obstructions on our journey. Their history? Gloria Miller reports that this (and likely some others that we will see) were built by Boy Scouts many years ago. I suspect it was deemed some kind of stream improvement project, probably with the fisheries habitat in mind.

A number of large homes became evident on the left side, although set well back from the river. There are more very large boulders. And a stream also comes in from the left. This is the Summers Drain, which extends south and east for several miles. An 1873 map of Clinton County shows a "Mill" at the mouth of this little stream, but I have no other information about such a structure. As I stared at another large maple, a whole flock of ducks took off from the river just ahead. I have never been very good at distinguishing species of ducks, but I can say that so far they have been rather nondescript, and therefore certainly not mallards or wood ducks.

I was facing another high bank ahead just to the left, meaning the river would be taking a right turn. At that very same point I encountered one of the largest boulders so far. This is a very picturesque long and gentle bend in the river, with the high bank accompanying us on the left, and many large rocks lining the river's edge at the bottom of the bank. For a short distance the river speeds up considerably, forming numerous ripples. After dropping away, a new bank arises on the left, again turning the river right, and again lined with even larger boulders at its base. I wedged my kayak between several of them, sat upon one, and ate a peaceful lunch. Back on the river, another large rock protrudes, fair warning that the ripples just ahead, which cross the entire stream, are caused by a shallow spot covered with cobblestones. We are now about a quarter mile from Francis Road. When you see the brownish log house appear straight ahead, a slight left bend, one more house, and a couple brief rapids will bring you to the Francis Road Bridge.

FRANCIS ROAD BRIDGE

Unlike the others, this bridge is not labeled. However, you can recognize Francis Road bridge as a flat concrete structure, with a single concrete rail forming little concrete "windows." Beyond the bridge, the left bank again rises somewhat. It is bordered below with lots of large boulders, and on its upper edge a rustic, log-topped fence. As I paused at the river's edge to check my map and notes, I noted the tracks of a deer which had come down to the river to drink.

A few more big rocks and then the river narrowed, giving me a short burst of speed until it widened out again. Then I surprised the second great blue heron of the day. A house appears on the right, and this is when you will see what is clearly the very largest boulder in the entire river. It must be some eight feet in length! Happily, it is very easily avoided.

Several more rapids follow in the shallows. Perhaps at this point I should clarify my use of the word "rapids." In all fairness, most kayakers and canoeists would call these "ripples." Rapids, technically I suppose, would mean genuinely fast water tumbling and splashing over rocks. However, I choose to call them rapids. Even if minor, for me a small rush of adrenalin is generated when approaching and passing over them.

A home appeared on the right, and then many more, all the way to Herbison Road. From one of them, a wooden stairway leads down to the river plain, and soon afterward Forest Hill Road comes down to the river's edge on the left and parallels the river. This is a good place to point out that the naming of this road has nothing to do with either a "forest" or a "hill." Rather, it is the proper name of early settler, Mr. Forrest Hill.

Another rock dam spans the river here, presently just below the surface. A dirt bank indicates that this is a popular put-in and take-out spot just south of Herbison. It apparently lies within the road right-of-way, and pull-off spots for your vehicle are adjacent. Discussion is underway involving several Clinton County governmental agencies to develop a formal public access site near here.

HERBISON ROAD BRIDGE # 1

This bridge, constructed in 2011, is a flat concrete structure, its sides consisting of three black horizontal railings and attached ornamentation which looks like a black picket fence. It is also unusual in that a number of planters have been placed along the railing, each sustaining bright red and white petunias. A placard in each indicates that they are placed in commemoration of a loved one who has passed on. The baskets are sponsored by the Looking Glass Garden Club, which also provides the ones at Herbison # 2, Wacousta and Bauer Road bridges. The Club was organized in 2009 with 20 charter members. Their primary focus is reforestation within the Looking Glass River corridor and stabilization and enhancement of the riparian buffer zone. And of course – beautification. Several other organizations are cooperators and Watertown Charter Township has supplied some project funding.

This is also believed to be the general location of an Indian Trail crossing between the DeWitt and Niles Indian settlements. This doesn't appear unreasonable, as there are some nearby areas of high ground and small hills.

On a previous occasion observing this location, there had been a heavy rain the day before, and the water of the Looking Glass was very uncharacteristic, being a muddy milk chocolate color. This is probably an indication and valuable reminder of the degree of runoff still flowing directly into the river, or via county drains accepting the topsoil from many farms.

*****

► **We've looked at a number of examples of the lives of the earliest settlers and pioneers along the Looking Glass. This time let's move forward just a few generations and listen to another version of early days near this particular site. Gloria Miller shared her childhood memories of the 1930s:**

As a youth I played in and on the river with neighbor kids. A favorite summer family outing was loading up the model A with frying pan and fishing poles, driving down a farm lane to the river bend and fishing for our supper. Water for coffee was dipped from a nearby spring.

One summer day my cousins and I launched a fallen tree in the river, straddled it and started paddling downstream. Shortly we were attacked by a colony of ants. We quickly abandoned ship and dog-paddled to shore.

In the winter, a weekend pastime was spearing fish through the ice. We kids would drive the fish downstream by pounding on the ice with poles to the men who had chopped holes in the ice. At day's end the pile of fish was divided between families. It was depression years and we could use the fish. Another winter activity was cutting blocks of ice from the river, which were stored in a neighbor's icehouse in sawdust. It was used in summer in our iceboxes to keep food cool. ◄

As you contemplate what such activities might have been like in times past at this location, I will move on under the first bridge. Immediately, a huge brick house faced me up on the right bank. There would be no others until I reached the second Herbison bridge. A turtle slid off yet another big boulder as I approached, and a heron left the water just beyond. At a point on the right where another bank joins the river, a small stream, the Cutler Drain, flows in at its base. There are a few more rapids, but as we progress along this section the boulders and rocks diminish, and the river returns to better representing its namesake. The bottom is largely coarse sand and fine gravel. When I flushed the heron one more time, it finally figured out that it could avoid my disturbances by simply flying back upstream instead. That was the last I saw of it.

Just before encountering a small island, I found Watertown Township's "Heritage Park," complete with a very fine canoe landing, on the right. While otherwise unmarked, it is readily noted by its straight outlines and gray color. It also supplies parking, restrooms, a pavilion, picnic facilities, playgrounds, and a sports complex. Road access is from Wacousta Road, behind the Watertown Charter Township office building. If you're just passing through, are hungry, and don't mind a short walk, hike up the access road to Wacousta, then turn left for about 0.2 miles. At the southeast intersection of Herbison and Wacousta, is the "Wacousta General Store." More about that a little later.

Back on the water, there is immediately that small island with a pretty little willow tree at its head. Follow the right channel, and the second Herbison Road bridge comes into view, the river having made a roughly one-mile loop in the meantime. This bridge, too, is adorned with planters filled with bright petunias.

HERBISON ROAD BRIDGE # 2

Moving on, and until the three-stall garage is sighted straight ahead, the river bottom has continued its sand and gravel mix. But beyond that, it transitions back to cobblestone and large rocks. Before long, I could hear the sound of rushing water. It was quite loud, and I soon spotted a rapids spanning the entire river. And this time I do mean "rapids." I approached carefully, and also took note on the right, nearly obscured by a tangle of logs, a stagnant channel leading inland. I had researched this earlier, but right now I needed to pay close attention to the river, and so will delay the telling of that story. This rapids is formed by a big pile of large stones across much of the river. Caution is advised. While shallow at the moment, a vessel could very easily be tipped. No sooner is this rapids passed than another appears, swifter and noisier that the first. It is also more dangerous; iron pipes are set at intervals across the river. A crumbling concrete structure is adjacent on the right bank. The water drop here is slightly greater than the first rapids, and again large rocks threaten to jostle the kayaker. It's shallow in this season, but again be careful.

A natural and smaller rapids follows, and a log which that day was occupied by three large turtles. A higher bank lies straight ahead, and the river accordingly turns to the right. A pile of large boulders on the left marks another rapids. A few more minor ones follow until the township park appears. Don't be misled by a gravelly site on the left; it is not the take-out. Rather it is just beyond the observation deck, being another simple concrete step-structure on the left. There are also a picnic pavilion and various recreation facilities. Toilet buildings are located across the ball field, near the basketball court. On December 18 of 2017 this park was rededicated as the Gloria Miller Looking Glass Valley Park, a most fitting tribute to her tireless efforts on behalf of the river and the community.

From this park north to the Wacousta General Store is only a quarter-mile jaunt.

※ THE WACOUSTA VICINITY ※

And so ... we've reached historic Wacousta. I will briefly tell its story, and also go back to try to explain the two special rapids and other remnants that we passed just upstream.

▶ **A number of settlers attempting to reach points farther westward along the Pontiac-Grand River Trail began to make their way into Watertown Township near the present site of Wacousta in 1837. They focused here at the point where the Looking Glass completes its northern loop and has returned south to cross the present Herbison Road again. Of course, at that time, there were no roads and no bridges. Essential supplies were initially brought down the Looking Glass by boat from Captain Scott's store in DeWitt.**

A small group of the settlers, however, saw great prospects. Together they purchased key properties near the river and quickly formed the "Waterloo Joint Stock Company," whose stated goals were to lay out a town and sell lots. The Looking Glass ran south for some distance on the east side of the proposed village. Just south of town, it made a sharp loop back on itself to the north. At this location the entrepreneurs saw an opportunity for, what seemed to me, a somewhat unusual means for establishing and operating a sawmill and gristmill. An early resident, Cornelia Daniells, eldest daughter of one of those in the eventual chain of owners of the sawmill, points out in her memoirs that the "many sharp curves and circuitous flowing of the Looking Glass River at this point" made it suitable for mill power.

But it was not a typical "dam-on-a-river." Instead, with what must undoubtedly have been an intense input of labor, they dug a canal across this riverbend to shortcut the longer loop that the river followed. This was the "stagnant channel" I referred to earlier. Just how this was all arranged and able to work was somewhat of a mystery. We have the testimony of a few early settlers in written records and maps, and also a number of clues remaining on the site today. It was time for a little detective work.

QUESTION # 1 – WHY DIG A SEPARATE CHANNEL?

Past testimony

I have found no reference whatsoever regarding the digging of a channel, nor of course the reason for this action. Since early maps show the channel in place and depict the mills located upon it, its intended purpose was obviously to serve as a "mill race," the channel through which water was funneled to provide power for the mills.

Present clues

By observation, the mill race was obviously artificially created, being relatively straight, and with earthen berms piled up on either side. Evidence of a small dam remains in the race.

Conclusion

I considered some possible explanations. The channel is less than half the length of the bypassed portion of the river. Yet the water of course drops the same distance. By dropping the level over a shorter distance, the current is faster and stronger in the mill race, the better to turn the wheels of the mills. There may be an even stronger reason to use a separate channel. It would be far easier to dig a channel and to construct a dam <u>within</u> the channel, and a mill <u>on</u> the channel, if it were at first kept closed at each end, than to dam the entire width of a significant fast-running river, and attempt to install structures there.

QUESTION # 2 – HOW DID THE MILL RACE ACQUIRE SUFFICIENT HEAD OF WATER TO POWER THE MILL?

What remains of the mill race today is all on the east side of Wacousta Road, and runs through property now owned by the Holiday Haven Girl Scouts. The westerly end of the channel has been blocked off just before it reaches Wacousta Road, and is recognizable by the raised bank on the right just before you pass under the bridge.

Aside from the accelerated drop of water, I was still baffled by what kind of hydraulic principles would enable this short-cutted channel system to work very well. Often an entire river or stream would be dammed to back up sufficient water and provide the necessary head to operate a mill.

Past Testimony

There had definitely been a dam somewhere here, as several writings make reference to it. Records show that in 1848 Nathaniel Daniells, one of the subsequent owners, proceeded to "repair the dam," and also bring it to a higher level, increasing the head and water power. But how would sufficient head be developed in the mill race, if almost the entire river was allowed to rush on by the channel opening and move on south within its original banks? Was there also a dam on the Looking Glass itself?

The early maps do indicate a widening of the Looking Glass just above this site, often an indication of a dam's backwaters. With one exception, however, they do not denote any semblance of a dam on the river. That exception is the 1873 atlas of Watertown Township. When we zoom in on the Wacousta area, we can see a very <u>distinct</u> widening of the river above a <u>bold straight line</u> drawn just below the channel entrance. It is not labeled, but very suggestive of a dam located at that point.

Present clues

Even today, there remains a slight widening of the river at this point. But might that have simply been a natural feature, in no way related to the operations just downstream? I needed to do an on-the-ground search of the river bank. Across the race from the Girl Scout office, at the far eastern tip of land bordering the river, I found what I was looking for. About 100 feet south of the entrance to the mill race from the river was a concrete sidewall, and an attached large block of concrete with numerous embedded rocks. From here extending out across the river were a series of 4-inch metal pipes driven into the river at regular intervals. It was these pipes which I cautioned should be avoided at the point of the second, bigger rapids.

Conclusion
This structure gives evidence of at least a low dam or a wing dam built out into the Looking Glass River. Usually such dams were adjustable for the amount of water they wanted to divert into the mill race, as opposed to that which they allowed to just past over or by into the river.

In a later conversation with Gloria Miller, who grew up in the area, this conclusion was verified. Gloria remembered the dam while it was still in place on the river, at the location I have noted, and being a concrete structure extending fully across the river. Obviously, it was removed or washed away sometime later.

QUESTION # 3 – WHERE WAS THE SAWMILL SITUATED?

Past Testimony
The sawmill was built in 1837. On an 1873 map of the Wacousta settlement, it is shown on the <u>south</u> edge of the canal, and reportedly about 15 rods (250 feet) east of Wacousta Road. However, another map shows it on the <u>north</u> edge of the canal. A third source, a narrative, places it <u>near</u> the mill race. Still a fourth narrative source says it sat <u>over</u> the mill race. A fifth depiction is in the 1873 map of Wacousta Township, which depicts the mill setting fully <u>across</u> the mill race.

Present clues
These last two sources seem the most likely and accurate descriptions, as then portions of it would have stood over both sides of the canal, and those other depictions on either the north or south side would simply have been a matter of the mapmaker's choice and convenience. The remains of a concrete structure can in fact be found in the mill race at about the 15-rod distance east of the road. Clearly placed to form an angle inward from both sides, they would have forced the water into a narrower passageway, where its speed and power would be increased.

Examining the southern berm of the mill race at the location of this concrete site provides additional evidence. It is clear that the mill could not have been located south of the race, nor could it be accessed from that side. The berm is very narrow, and drops immediately down to a marshy area, flooded in any time of high water.

Conclusion

The sawmill sat <u>over</u> the mill race and was accessed from the north.

*****

With these issues presumably settled, we should note that soon after the sawmill, a gristmill was added at the far downstream end of the mill race, which originally did not rejoin the Looking Glass until just <u>after</u> it had passed under the old bridge. This mill was constructed just west of Wacousta Road, but in this case clearly on the north bank of the race. Today that site is also owned by the Girl Scouts, and a rustic sign marks the approximate spot of the old mill. The *History of Clinton County*, 1880, tells us that until the construction of the gristmill, some of the early settlers of Eagle Township had traveled down the Looking Glass, took their grain to the gristmill at Portland, and brought back their flour and meal, all by canoe.

Within the mill race itself there were thus probably two small dams. Records tell us that "the mill race furnished the power for both mills." One would have been at the sawmill site, where the narrowing concrete wings still remain. The other would have to have been at the far end of the canal, in order to provide a second head of water for the gristmill. In fact, an account by Julie (Staines) Peters recalls herself "swimming down by the old (grist) mill," and that her uncle as a child "was caught in the undertow where the water came over the mill." Fortunately, he was hauled out by his brother, but the words "over the mill" indicate higher water behind a dam spilling into the river, creating the dangerous undercurrents as the canal water rejoined the river.

*****

A boarding house and store soon followed the mills, and the company worked to interest other "mercantile enterprises" to set up their businesses there. It was first called Waterloo, after the company name. However, the envisioned development was not very successful, and the investments changed hands several times in rapid succession. By 1848, the company was essentially defunct. An independent interest consisting of Nathaniel I. and Nelson Daniels took over in that year and rebuilt both of the mills, which were already entering a state of decay, and opened a store. Also in operation were a general store, a market with grocery store, a drug/grocery, a boot/shoe/grocery, two blacksmith shops, and a millinery. There were lawyers and physicians also in residence.

In spite of a small number of commercial buildings getting underway, the area around Wacousta remained on the verge of wilderness. Indian visits remained common for a time, as they had around the DeWitt settlement. They camped along the river and hunted and fished in the area. Their furs and other products were brought to the Wacousta stores and bartered for other goods.

According to her memoir, Cornelia Daniells (later married name Hazard), having traveled the Erie canal with her family, arrived in Wacousta on January 9 of 1849, at the age of 15. The very next day she was approached by the school director and asked to be the teacher in their new school. She was to be paid $1.50 per week for a term of eight weeks. After some amount of persuasion, she accepted. Her report goes on to describe the surrounding countryside at that time. I have excerpted a number of words and phrases descriptive of the still primitive surroundings:

> *As was the custom in those days, the teacher "boarded round." Everyone received the teacher eagerly and with cordiality and gave her the best they had. When a storm came in the night and caught me at the farther distances, the host would take his steers and sled to carry scholars and teacher to school.*
>
> *... exceeding newness of the country*
>
> *Here and there a log cabin or shanty, and all the rest dense woods of large trees, many of them gigantic.*
>
> *North of the Center ... we struck into solid woods, the road winding through among the trees to the Hunter bridge.*

...between our two bridges to the east of here, not a clearing.

Not a tree was cut or road west of the Center corners to the river north and nearly to Mr. Lowell's south. Half a mile north of Wacousta one came to solid woods extending nearly six miles.

As she had often heard her father remark:

To settle up a new wooded country took the people back a generation towards barbarism.

By now, however, it had been determined that another town in Michigan had already selected the name of "Waterloo," and to keep the mail service clear, it had been necessary to determine a new name for the village. According to the most popular account, one of the settlers suggested "Wacousta," the name of an Indian maiden who was said to have served as an informant, warning the garrison stationed at the fort in Detroit of an impending attack by her tribe in 1763.

As I hinted at earlier, however, one later source suggested it may have derived from an Indian word for "sluggish river." That account comes from James Calder, a pioneer of Olive Township, as told to T. H. Townsend. I once again called upon the local expert in the Native language, Alphonse Pitawanakwat, to determine whether "Wacousta" might be an alternative Indian name for another characteristic of the river, it's slow-moving current, or "sluggish waters." He concluded that no such name or resemblance was applicable to the Anishinaabe language. He suggested that if true, it might possibly have been verbiage from another tribe, such as the Mohawk, a few of whose members were sometimes intermixed in the area. The other and more likely explanation is that Wacousta has nothing to do with the river itself, and that the maiden story holds firm. In either case, the name was accepted and remains to this day.

*****

Plans in 1868 and 1880 to consider a railroad route near Wacousta came to naught. In 1906, the settlement had 300 residents, a bank, two churches, several retail stores, foundry, other merchants, creamery plant, and physicians. In the 1940s the dam on the channel broke and was not replaced. Julie Peters, aforementioned, recalled also that "the island," that is the area encircled by the channel and the river bend was often used by area youngsters as a ballfield. Gloria Miller adds that it was the site of community events and holiday celebrations such as the 4th of July. It remains open and of higher ground to this day, located just across the old channel from the Scout office, and used as their campground.

Earlier, reference was made to the Wacousta General Store. It is situated on the same site as the original general store built by Benjamin Silsbee in 1847. The current structure, while not that same building, is still cited as being the oldest building remaining in the community. Portions of it exceed 100 years of age. Mr. Walt Nickel, in a newspaper article written many years ago, related that according to the owners at that time, the Kraft's, "The original building, which is part of the present store, was situated on the banks of the Looking Glass River…it was an Indian trading post in its early years. The timbers, some of which are visible in the present store, were all hand hewn. About 1890 the building was moved to its present site, and later on further additions were made." Several additional changes in ownership were also made over the decades. Current owners are Dennis and Shelly Jegla. They retain the motto of previous owners: "everything from soup to nuts," and it is worth a visit. They are open from 8 to 9 almost every day of the year. ◄

✻ ON THE RIVER: TRIP SIX ✻
(Wacousta to Hinman)

WACOUSTA ROAD BRIDGE

The website HistoricBridges.org lists this bridge as a Metal Stringer (Multi-Beam), Fixed style of 86 feet in length, built in 1955 (our familiar flat concrete structure). Their comment: "this is an unaltered example of a typical mid-20th century bridge in Michigan." It remains in use today, with double side rails of galvanized metal. Petunias again grace the side rails.

For the first mile beyond Wacousta, the river flows within a distinctly deeper valley and with narrower adjacent marsh. This condition was obviously noticed by later developers. A road closely parallels both sides of the river, and each is lined with houses. It is the most intensely developed mile of river in the entire system. Fortunately, however, the deepness of the valley, and the still-frequent adjacent narrow wetlands, most often place them on hilltops far back from the river and not visible to the summer boater. The visible houses would alternate between left and right banks until near Bauer Road, when they would become apparent on both banks. In spite of the intense development, this is a very peaceful and pretty segment of river.

Bonnie and I put in about noon on a mostly-sunny 68-degree day – very pleasant. A small rapids soon appeared, the first of many; this would be a very fun day. At the very first bend to the right, a cement abutment can be seen up on the left bank. This is apparently the outlet of the Openlander Drain. There will be several more rapids in this mile and occasional big boulders. The bottom, however, is rather free of stones and looks good for wading. We spotted several small schools of fat minnows of some kind.

HARLOW'S LIVERY – THE ONE AND ONLY

Near the end of this mile, still within this deeper-than-usual valley, the river has temporarily slowed and become very peaceful again. Houses are visible for a time up on both hillsides. We can see Bauer Road bridge up ahead. It is another flat concrete bridge, built in 2000, with a heavy wooden beam rail along each side. Until recently, on the left and just before the bridge, you would have seen Harlow's Wacousta Canoe Livery, the only commercial livery on the entire river. It was begun by Betty J. Harlow during the early 1970s, inspired by watching canoeists frequently pass by her house. After several decades of service to river enthusiasts, Betty died in late 2015, and the livery business no longer exists. We await news as to whether another entrepreneur will take up the business. In the meantime, by the grapevine I am hearing that one or more other businesses are now providing service to parts of the Looking Glass.

BAUER AND WRIGHT ROAD BRIDGES

There was one more encounter as we neared the Bauer Road bridge. Something was hanging in a low tree branch about one foot above the water. As I moved over to investigate, sliding by just a few feet away, I saw that it was a hornets' nest, and it was occupied! This would not be a good situation in which to disturb a nest of hornets.

A fair-sized rapids (for the Looking Glass) comes up just past this bridge, also adorned with petunia planters. While protruding boulders are infrequent here, there are numerous others setting just below the surface, ready to rock your boat. There will be one house immediately on the left, and then a pretty wild stretch nearly to Wright Road. It is not until then that cobblestone begins to increase on the bottom, more big boulders appear, and with them, the inevitable rapids. I could hear Wright Road traffic just ahead. When you spot several homes high up on the right bank, the bridge is just around the corner. There is no sign on the bridge, nor any more of the attractive petunia boxes. It is a flat concrete structure with a heavy concrete railing.

THE NILES SETTLEMENT

Not long after passing Wright Rd, the Husted-Landenburg drain enters the river. In its natural form, it had been a small stream which would in time take the name Niles Creek. After the recent dry spell, its exit to the river was hardly noticeable. Only a small trickle ran down through a very muddy side bank. It looks as though the opening is rather wide, though vegetation at the moment hides much of it. It is also near here, perhaps a bit nearer to the upcoming subdivision of large homes on Eden Trail which will come into view up on the left hillside, that the Niles-Groger party had abandoned their raft. Up where Niles Creek crosses Clark Road, the nearby north-south road is also named Niles.

Obviously, it is now time to return to the story of the Niles-Groger party, which was earlier introduced as we continued westerly upon departing DeWitt. We noted there that after abandoning their raft near today's Eden Trail subdivision, they continued their journey to Portland the next day. Actually, that leaves out an important part of the story.

▶ **Mr. Niles had camped that night near the present northern terminus of Niles Road. The next morning his departure was delayed as one of his cows had wandered off during the night. It was afternoon before he could continue on his way, but in the meantime he had gotten a good look at the countryside, and had greatly admired both the land and the little stream (the future Niles Creek) that flowed nearby. Although he continued with the party to Portland, he decided**

98

he had not found any site along the way that was any more to his liking than the prior campsite where he lost his cow.

Thus it was that he purchased 80 acres which today would give one quarter mile of frontage on the south side of Clark Road, and one half mile of frontage on the east side of Niles Road, with the favored creek running north through all of it. He built a very large cabin there, measuring 28 by 30 feet. Being along a main route for other westward-seeking travelers who would follow, he frequently and cheerfully provided overnight shelter. One pioneer woman, Harriet Munro, compared his hospitality to Scott's in DeWitt, stating, "Another regular stopping place was owned by Mr. and Mrs. Niles who had been there long enough to be known and who were always ready to help new settlers." Apparently this helpful sentiment was not uncommon among the earliest strugglers in the wilderness. She goes on to say, "Wherever there was an inhabitant we found hospitality. We were never obliged to go farther for accommodations. We were asked to share with them what they had." When the Munro's own cabin was completed, the family was gathered up for the trip:

> *After three weeks' time father came for us. The rains had raised the Looking Glass River so that it could not be forded. We were all taken across the river in an Indian canoe. A pole was used instead of a paddle. We enjoyed the drive through the woods. It was night when we arrived at the Niles settlement, but there was a large living room and a blazing wood fire.*

The Niles cabin also served as a gathering place for churchgoers, and with its great fireplace and smooth floors, a place for social dances. Other settlers and activities apparently also gravitated to the general area, and it became unofficially referred to as the "Niles settlement."

Niles Creek had enough flow to power a small mill, as evidenced by its considerable springtime current and volume yet today. Whether the mill was located on the Niles property, or closer to the Looking Glass is not clear. A cemetery became established near the Niles property, perhaps originating as the family's personal burying ground. At least eight members of the Niles family are buried there, and as of today, nearly 500 others, including several whose names now are forever applied to other roads in the vicinity. It is located on a pleasant grassy knoll on the west side of Niles Road, about one tenth mile south of Clark Road.

While the Niles settlement never established itself as an organized community, back then it was clearly the focal point for newly-arriving pioneers, neighboring settlers, and early social gatherings. ◄

WILDERNESS LIFE

► While we're on the subject, let's take just a moment or two to learn a little more about what it took to live as a wilderness family in those days. First, of course, as we've already seen, a family member had to explore the mostly roadless wilderness to locate a potential homesite to meet their needs. Another trip was required to reach a government land office and record a deed. Then it was a return to the newly-purchased property, to haul in supplies and prepare it for the family. Home-seekers today buy a completely finished house with a fully landscaped yard. In these modern times, it is therefore difficult for us to imagine the efforts once required. To help us out, let's listen to the account of several early pioneers. One of these is Henry Rowland (HR), who built his homestead "on the south bank of the Looking Glass," in about 1838. Another pioneer of the early 1830's, John Nowlin (JN), even though farther east, and not on the Looking Glass, provides additional pertinent descriptions in his book, *The Bark Covered House*. Still another was Harriet Munro (HM, married name Longyear), previously mentioned, whose parents settled in the watershed in 1836. And finally, we will hear from Mrs. N. B. Rice (NBR), an early resident of Portland near the mouth of the Looking Glass.

Accessing the New Homesite (most being well off the principal Indian trails)

HM: (late 1830s) First of all, just to get to their own new cabin, her father *was obliged to make a road from the Niles settlement to his land, about six miles...*

JN: *The next thing ... was clearing a road through a black ash swale ... cleared out the old logs and brush, then felled trees lengthwise toward each other, sometimes two together...He cut logs twelve feet long and laid them side by side across the center of the road ... We called this our corduroy road...When it was still I could hear a cart or wagon, coming or going, rattling and pounding over the logs for nearly a mile."*

Building the Home

JN: Father *"then cut black ash trees* (and) *peeled off the bark to roof his* (log) *house."*

HR: *I then went to work to build me a house; cut the logs, hewed the ends a little, and piled them up house shape; made the roof of bark; split some logs in two and laid the flat sides up for a floor; took the boards from one of our goods boxes and patched up a door; built the indispensable fireplace of stones, with flatish ones laid for the hearth; built sides and back up the jams; put in the tramel with its hooks, and went on building the chimney back of stones, then farther up we built of sticks and clay to the top. He followed this up by building a bedstead, chairs, table and brooms.*

Keeping Warm

JN: The family had to *"use the utmost precaution"* not to let the fire go out. *"Sometimes I have known my little ... sister ... to go more than a quarter of a mile, to the Blare place* (a neighbor), *to borrow fire."*

NBR: Mrs. N. B. Rice observed similarly that *"before the day of matches ... it was common occurrence to see people going to the neighbors after a shovel of coals, for great care had to be taken lest the fire go out. A flint stone, a jack knife and a bunch of tow* (plant fibers) *were kept on hand by some for fear the fire would fail them entirely."*

Clearing the Land for Farming

JN: *No man, unless he has experienced it himself, can have an adequate idea of the danger and labor of clearing a farm in heavy, timbered land ... the walking, the chopping and sweating, the running and the dodging ... behind trees.*

HR: *I was anxious to get to chopping. It was no light task to clear the land of the heavy dense growth of timber upon it. We*

101

chopped about ten acres that first winter. In the spring our axes were pretty dull, for there was not a grindstone in the settlement, but we knew that an Englishman had one ten miles down the river.

Obtaining Basic Supplies

HM: *Father spent the winter in going to and from Detroit and Dexter for supplies, taking ten days or two weeks each trip.*

HR: *Captain Scott, near DeWitt, used to keep a supply of flour and pork, which he hauled up from Pontiac. I have known Stephen Groger (of the Niles-Groger party) to walk from his farm to Scott's, twelve miles or more, and do a day's work; would stay sometimes and work several days and take his pay in provisions, carrying them home on his back at night, after he had worked hard all day. One night I remember he brought 100 pounds of flour, a quarter of venison, and several other articles.*

Other Incidents of Life in a Primitive Land

HM: *... The sugar maple trees were tapped and maple syrup and sugar were plentiful. Several hundred pounds of sugar were made, which relieved one of the wants of a new country. Fish were plentiful, the men catching with dip-nets hundred of a night. All surplus was put into half barrels and salted for future use. Wild onions grew along the banks of our brook. In the fall wild-plums, crabapples and frost-grapes were plentiful. Honey was found in trees...and also bees-wax, which furnished us with wax candles ... Indians were friendly and always hungry. Their liking for white-man's bread was simply appalling. We bought venison of them whenever they brought it to us. We had no reason to fear them. They were always sober and peaceable."*

JN: *The wolves, also, were very common; we could often hear them at night ... One evening a Mr. Bruin (a bear) called at our house and stood erect at our north window ... One day, towards evening, mother was getting supper and heard a strange noise which seemed to come from a chest which stood in the back part of the room on legs ... they finally looked under the chest and there, to their astonishment, they saw a large black rattlesnake all curled up watching their movements.*

Of our first settlement, father did not feel safe; the string of the door latch was taken in, the door was fastened and blockaded on the inside, his ax and rifle were placed with care ... at the head of his bed. None of us knew what might happen before the light of another morning, for we were in a wilderness land, and neighbors were far apart. ◄

CONTINUING DOWNSTREAM

Now it is almost two <u>centuries</u> later, and as we continue on our far more modern river journey, we can scarcely imagine such conditions. Today, the general location is accessed by Eden Trail, where a significant modern subdivision exists high on the hillside. From the river, the first group of homes can be seen to have a big expanse of neatly mowed hillside sloping down to the river. Then the river swings momentarily away from the subdivision, only to return to another group of these homes just a little farther down.

We did note several large carp near here. But this is not the time or place to be mindlessly staring at the fish below or admiring the fine homes on the hillside. Instead, keep your eyes focused on the river ahead; it has some action in store for you! You can hear the first rapids from some distance away; it is probably the largest rock dam encountered thus far. All told, I counted at least a dozen sets of rapids in this section. And accompanying them were often many more of those large boulders. At one site in particular, we selected a route between two protruding boulders which formed the familiar "V" suggesting deeper water. Unfortunately, at the lower end of that "V" were several more, only slightly submerged boulders. "Good luck" missing all of them! There are so many rocks in this section that it became difficult whether to define the rapids as the result of man-made rock placements or natural groupings, such as might be found within the many gravel deposits in the area. I believe there were some of each. Don't be fooled by what might occasionally appear to be calm water just ahead. It won't last long before the sound of more rapids refocuses your attention. Just enjoy the ride! At today's late-season level there was frequent jostling of the kayak, and of hanging up briefly on the gravel bars. So let's agree to return again sometime to re-do this exciting section when there are about four more inches of water.

A pretty little stream came in from the left, stony-bottomed rather than the customary mud. A low streambank, although mowed by the uphill homeowner, tells us that Tallman Road is just ahead. Its bridge design is just like the one we passed at Wright Road.

We have been spotting some more larger fish – young bass, I believe. For a short while there is not a big rock in sight, but that won't last long. After passing a very high bank on the right with homes, the cobblestone bottom, large rocks just below the surface, and a few protruding larger boulders again make their presence known.

Just ahead, where a large brown house appears on the left, we spotted a major log jam ahead. We approached carefully, backpaddling our kayaks to maintain position as we searched diligently for the tiny opening that we felt sure the Friends would have cut through somewhere. But there was none. Glancing at the right bank, we noted a wooden structure sloping down into the water, from which led a well-worn path past large silver maples to another such structure just past the logjam. As we portaged this short trail, it was evident why the Friends had not cut a river path. The jam was a massive tangle of trees and limbs accumulated over time and many floods. It was far simpler to take this very convenient portage.

When you see a house high on the right bank with a stairway going all the way down to the water, several more rapids lay just ahead. As that settled back down to a welcome wide and lazy section, we noticed some pretty purplish-pink flowers just up the bank from the water's edge. It was the Joe Pye weed, a member of the sunflower family which can grow to as much as eight feet high. The Joe Pye plant was apparently used by a well-known New England Indian healer for various medicinal purposes. His Native name was … Jopi.

Be on the lookout now for the tall abutments of a prior bridge which once crossed at Hinman Road. If you're taking out here, as we did, the best place is the far side of the abutment, on the left side. By "best" I don't mean easy. The bottom is covered with cobblestones, making footing precarious. The walk up to the road is steep, but short.

✵ ON THE RIVER - TRIP SEVEN ✵
(Hinman to Howe)

While the bridge has been removed, the concrete abutments remain, very conspicuously edging in from both sides of the stream, and some 10-15 feet in height. It is a quiet spot, especially on the south side, with the road ending nearly at stream-side. There are no immediately adjacent homes nor manicured yards. So...is this a legal access for putting in or taking out watercraft? The Clinton County Road Commission believes it is. And the explanation offered by the Law Enforcement Division, as we discussed earlier, suggests the same, since the road itself and its right-of-way actually extend to the river's edge.

In any case, my son Todd and I reached this point at about 3 PM on a Saturday, this time using it as a put-in place. The dead-end turn-around suffices for parking, and it is a reasonable, though rather steep take-down to the water. Remember that the river bottom at this point consists of rather large stones, making walking in the river to enter your kayak rather challenging. In addition, numerous very large boulders begin again, protruding well above water level. They are very picturesque, especially on this pleasant and mostly sunny day. Almost immediately some small bass appeared, and farther down some larger ones mixed in. Carp, or maybe suckers, also showed up in small schools at several locations. These were the most numerous fish yet encountered on the Looking Glass. Just down from Hinman appeared what seemed to be another rock dam, with a row of large rocks extending well across the river.

▶ **It wasn't long before the traffic on Grange Road could be heard. As it neared, we were keeping in mind the *History of Clinton and Shiawassee Counties* which says that there was once a sawmill on the Looking Glass, east (upstream) of present day Grange Road. That means that somewhere soon there would have to have been another dam. It may have been on the main river. It may have been on an incoming tributary. Or perhaps it was a separated mill-race of the design we found back at Wacousta. It was again time to look for clues.**

As the bridge comes nearer, the left bank juts abruptly out into the river, which then makes a very sharp bend around it to the left. The jut itself seemed to be artificially raised, which would be consistent with the construction of a dam here on the river. Also at the point of jutting, a bunch of large boulders were piled on the left

bank, and there were what appeared to be sawn timbers lying parallel with the current across the bottom. The river itself was also deeper and wider here, as might be expected where a dam and its millpond had once existed.

If, as it appeared, this was the dam site, where had the mill been situated and how was it operated? The best clue of all was waiting just around the corner. First, we needed to pass by a small island. Take the right branch – the left is a very shallow rapids. But before passing under the Grange Road bridge, a smaller but significant channel joins the main river from the left. We examined it closely, and by all appearances it is the old mill-race cutting across the riverbend. I had not spotted the upstream end of the race where it left the river, but it obviously would have been somewhat upstream of the jutting left bank we had just passed. The layout of this entire site was highly reminiscent of the Wacousta site, and so probably operated in the same manner. The mill would have been here, somewhere along the cut-through channel. The main dam would in that case have extended across the full river at the point of the jutting, thereby diverting sufficient water into the mill-race at it upper end, to power the sawmill.

Sometime subsequent to this on-site investigation, Jeanne Bewersdorff, local historian, provided me with the welcome lead confirming all of this. George W. McCrumb was the early owner of some 220 acres on both the north and south sides of the Looking Glass, and both the east and west sides of Grange Road. He built a sawmill, and gathered much of his timber from his own surrounding lands. Not only is his ownership confirmed by the 1896 Map of Eagle Township, but it also clearly identifies his sawmill on the southern bank of the Looking Glass, just east of Grange. Ms. Bewersdorff also uncovered and shared an 1881 drawing of the sawmill and the nearby bridge. In that drawing the separate mill race re-joining the river at this very point is quite obvious. This was a wonderful find! McCrumb also reached out to plat the village of Eagle, and was instrumental in building the railroad station, farmers elevator, and reportedly, even a local hotel. His name remains affixed to the county road just south of his sawmill. ◄

*****

With that issue solidly resolved, we then passed quietly under Grange Road, yet another bridge like the ones at Tallman and Wright. Slightly beyond the bridge are several homes up on the left hillside. There is another small island and a very large rock. The hill on the left here comes down to the river's edge and is very steep. More big rocks and more small rapids. For a while the river gets wider and shallower. Todd and I were seeing more and larger bass. We stopped for a snack, sitting upon a very large and flat-topped boulder in the left part of the river. We dubbed it "picnic rock."

There were more small rapids, but the very best so far was where the river made a rather sharp bend to the right. At this rapids, you could actually see the drop in the river, and the rapids extended for a longer distance than any of the others. If only the water had been just a few inches deeper to keep us from scraping bottom on some of the rocks, this would have been an exhilarating run!

THE EAGLE CANAL

Near here is also the site of the contemplated Eagle Canal and mill. Let me first set the stage. As should be evident by now, and will be further impressed as we progress downriver, in the early days of Michigan, not surprisingly, a river's worth was judged largely by its ability to support navigation and/or its potential to power mills. Without a local gristmill to grind grain into flour, or a sawmill to provide timbers for homes, barns and other structures, such essential commodities would have to be shipped long distances. This was both difficult, as we have already seen, and very expensive. Fortunately, as an 1840 writer observed at that time, "A great number of excellent mill-sites are to be found on the Shiawassee, Looking Glass and Maple Rivers, which could be profitably employed either in the manufacture of flour or lumber," two of the more critical products in the success of early settlements. Historic records and commentary suggest that not less than nine dams with associated grist or sawmills were located on the historic Looking Glass, or nearby on its tributary streams. Some 90,000 dams remain in the entire United States to this day.

As to water transportation, in addition to that available from naturally-flowing streams, considerable thought was given to artificially uniting river systems. One such plan was approved by the State legislature in 1837, and provided for a "survey of a canal route to unite the waters of the Saginaw River with…the Maple or Grand Rivers." Funding difficulties and the promise of railroads eventually doomed this and similar projects.

▶ A similar scheme had been developed on a more local basis on the Looking Glass. Here about three miles downstream from the site of the Niles/Groger party's raft abandonment, near the intersection of Eagle Township's Herbison and Patrick Roads, the Looking Glass and the Grand Rivers are only about two miles apart. This feature was noted by Marshal Meade and a Mr. Townsend, who owned lands between the two rivers. They also recognized that from this site the Grand River's course was nearly 40 miles to its junction with the Looking Glass downstream, whereas the Looking Glass route was only 10 miles from that juncture. Obviously then, the Looking Glass dropped much more rapidly from this point downstream, and there must consequently be a rather significant drop in elevation cross country between the two rivers at this location. John Mullett, who had in the 1820's served as one of the government surveyors establishing Michigan territory's land lines, was hired to survey the area. He found the elevation difference was in fact 21 feet. As Meade and Townsend anticipated, this was clearly an opportunity for establishing one of the most significant water-powers in the State, if only a canal could be dug between the two!

The Eagle survey had determined that indeed, the intervening ground was suitable for ditching, and the required cut of manageable depth. Just where was their contemplated starting point on the Looking Glass? A big river bend to the right is accompanied by a high bank all along the left (south) side, the direction of the Grand River. It is hard to imagine cutting through such an impediment in those days before modern excavating machinery. Consequently it is my opinion that the designers must have planned to use the section of riverbank just a short distance back upstream from this bend, where the banks give way to flatter land. Quite likely then, it may have coincided with the location of the present south-running Moyer Drain. Unfortunately, due to the unexpected death of Mr. Townsend, the plan was never carried through. It turns out that this is fortunate for us, however, as we can now continue our journey down the remaining miles of the Looking Glass! ◀

*****

And this is indeed a very enjoyable section of river: rapids, big boulders, fish, hills, wildness, and great scenery! Towards the end, a few houses appear on the left, with lawns extending down to the river's edge. Their frontage is completely lined with large stones, apparently placed there manually for protection from erosion. In the river itself, the really big boulders have now diminished greatly, and are in fact becoming rather scarce.

Howe Road bridge finally came into view. It stands well above the river in contrast to most other bridges we've seen, perhaps 15 to 20 feet in this low water season. Otherwise, it is again a flat concrete structure with a galvanized metal railing. Just before the bridge, there is a river exit on the left bank. A well-worn path leads to vehicle pullouts on both sides of the road along the west bridge approach. There was plenty of space for the three other cars parked there. However, the climb up the road embankment, though short, is very steep and strenuous, and the fine gravel surface rather slippery.

❋ ON THE RIVER – TRIP EIGHT ❋
(Howe to Cutler)

We had turned another page on the calendar before we were able to return to the river. It was Labor Day. Bonnie was on a separate outing, so perhaps spurred by my tales of this great adventure, my son, Tedd and his wife Jessica joined me instead. As thunderstorms were forecast for the afternoon, we got on the river before 10 AM.

This next section of river was said to be a pretty good smallmouth bass fishery. As already noted, in the prior river segment we had in fact been seeing more and larger bass. Throughout the day, we did see quite a few small bass, some in extensive schools, and maybe one keeper, but otherwise they were keeping pretty well out of sight.

Grange Road paralleled the river on the right for a short distance beyond our start. Some big rocks soon re-appeared, along with some minor rapids. The water is faster here, but also distinctly wider and shallower for much of the day, so that we frequently scraped bottom, and on more than one occasion, stepped out of our kayaks to walk them down to deeper water. One of the most difficult of such spots to navigate was right after a slow right turn. Farther on, the river would narrow again, forcing the water into a little greater depth, at times probably around 30 inches. At one point the right the bank rises exceptionally high right from the river's edge, the highest bank we've yet seen. Visible houses are again few and far between in this section.

Wildlife made their appearances at various points. Soon after our start a muskrat was struggling its way upstream for some reason known only to him (or her). The usual herons were also there. But at one point, Tedd hollered for my attention to a bird in flight just ahead of us in the river channel. It was large and had a beautiful white tail – a bald eagle! Our location was Eagle Township, after all. Next there were two turtles trying to settle onto a sunny spot on this only partly sunny day. A two-foot snake swam across the river between us; just how a snake can swim is amazing to me!

Some of the vegetation we were seeing was interesting as well. In the stream itself we took note of the very long strands of green "seaweed," always lined up with the current. Well, they weren't actually seaweed. Tedd "Googled" it right on the spot and found it was "string algae." String algae is made up of cylindrical cells which are connected end to end, thus forming these long green hair-like strands. They can be many feet long, as I found was the case when one became entangled around my paddle.

A dainty orange and yellow flower on a slender bush-like plant grew in occasional patches, sometimes right out on a log jam where just enough mud had accumulated. As there is of course no lack of poison ivy along the river, it is well to learn more about this jewelweed. According to altnature.com, it "has been used for centuries in North America by Native Americans and Herbalists, as a natural preventative and treatment for poison ivy … and many other skin disorders."

We were also seeing increasing numbers of a tall, yellow daisy-like flower. "Google" again came to our aid, identifying it as sunchoke or Jerusalem artichoke. It is in fact related to the sunflower family. And as the name implies, its tuber (root) is edible as a vegetable. It is sometimes grown domestically and commercially for that purpose.

Wild grape vines are prolific in this part of Michigan, and the river is no exception. At one point we passed under hanging vines reaching down nearly to the river. Tedd went over to investigate the supporting tree and found that the vine, at its on-shore source, was at least seven inches in diameter!

SOME SPECIAL TREES

The Sycamores – Blotchy Giants

Along the river banks, we've also begun to see some interesting trees, among them the sycamores. They are readily recognized by their blotchy bark, showing mottled patches in shades of brown, creamy white and olive green, especially in the upper branches. How does this happen? As the sycamore ages, patches of its outer layers of bark begin to drop off, revealing the vari-colored inner bark layers.

There was a big overhanging sycamore on the left just as we departed the Howe Road put-in. And just before Monroe Road, on the right, are a couple more nice specimens. The best one of all that day, however, was a huge, gnarled tree on the right bank. It was mostly hollowed out up to 8 or 10 feet, and Tedd was easily able to stand inside. There will be some more enormous specimens down at the mouth at the take-out point. Amongst the largest of Michigan's trees, the current state champion measures more than eight feet in diameter!

The Tamaracks - A Most Unusual Conifer

When you have passed a major and tricky log jam near the end of today's journey, keep your eyes trained to the right. There, along a somewhat open marshy area you will spot some unusual pine-like trees with lacy, seaweed-like foliage. But it is not a pine. And while it is a conifer, it is not an evergreen. Instead, it is the tamarack, or eastern larch. Every autumn its needles turn bright yellow or orange, and then drop off until spring. It was once a common tree of southern Michigan swamplands, and was often mentioned by the original surveyors in the 1820s and 30s, and as we've seen, even more so by later travelers and settlers of Eagle and DeWitt townships. The chronicler of the 1906 *Past and Present History of Clinton County* tells us that the property of the early settler of the Chandler Farm bordering Bath and DeWitt townships consisted originally of "800 acres of oak-opening uplands, 500 acres of marsh meadow, and 600 acres of tamarack swamp!" Early woodland clearing and drainage of the swamps has greatly reduced its distribution. Known for its rot resistance, the tamarack was widely used in early days for timbers in barns and houses, many of which continue to serve their initial purpose to this day. My father-in-law's barn, built in 1917, included tamarack rafters from his own swampland and are as sturdy as ever, some with bark still attached.

Of course, it is not only the tamarack species that has been reduced within the watershed over the last couple centuries. For better or worse, and probably some of each, so effective have been the draining, ditching, clearing, filling, and developing that 75% of the wetlands which faced the first pioneers to pass through this watershed in the 1830s are no longer wet. So persistent has been the clearing, farming, settlement, transportation systems and urbanization that 80% of the original area of forest cover is no longer forested. Within the watershed, at least 34 living species have now been classified as endangered, threatened, or of special concern, and could face elimination. About half of these are rare plants, and the other half rare animal-types. Certainly we need to be more conscientious and careful with our precious watershed.

Adding Color

Driving out to our Howe Road put-in today, we had noted a number of sumacs turning their familiar autumn red. We'd also been seeing occasional maples along the river putting on their red attire, even though autumn was still a month away. Later the entire river in some sections would be arched over in the reds of sugar and red maples; the yellows of silver maples, ashes and hickories; and tones of purple, gold and copper displayed by oaks and beech. What gives them these brilliant colors; where do they come from?

As I explained in my other book, *Ancient Forests: Trees and Timber in Bible Lands and Times*, the green associated with summer leaves is due to their sun-generated chlorophyll content. But subdued below this dominance are lesser concentrations of the other colors. When autumn approaches, days shorten and less sugar is produced. In addition, the tree produces a layer of special cork cells at the point where each leaf attaches to the twig, effectively cutting off the supply of water to each leaf. When this happens, the chlorophyll breaks down first, allowing the underlying brilliant colors of autumn to show forth in a scene most pleasing to the eye.

*****

All of this discussion should not suggest that this stretch of river is totally a lazy one. Not long after beginning today, the river had bent to the left, and we were faced with the distant view of many, many large boulders in the river. There are several rapids in succession, with large rocks also to be seen (or just felt) beneath the water. A fish of some size jumped here, too.

A bit later another straight-ahead view of the river occurred, revealing an exceptionally large single rock. It is essentially flat-topped, and I suppose we should call it "picnic rock # 2." Just beyond this single rock are two other large boulders near mid-stream. Fortunately the river is deeper here, and pointing your kayak right between them gives a momentary thrill as you pass safely through on a noticeable downhill. A house is also straight ahead, but the stream takes a sharp right to avoid it. There is a nice deep pool at this spot. When you next look up you can see a bridge ahead. A sign on its side confirms "Monroe Road."

MONROE ROAD BRIDGE

A number of years ago, the bridge at Monroe Road was listed on the MDOT website of Michigan's Historic Bridges. The accompanying photo showed a very dilapidated but still very picturesque iron truss bridge with many missing wooden decking planks. It was built in 1894, and at 148 feet in length, was one of the longest Pratt through truss bridges in the State. It had already been closed to traffic in 1980, but wasn't removed until 2002, when replaced by the new concrete structure seen there now. It is the same simple design as that at Wright, Tallman and Grange.

Beyond that a very pretty little stream slides in from the right. Clear water is flowing freely. I'd like to think it is a natural stream, but I suppose that in some parts it, like nearly all others, is part of a county drain. From my map, I'd conclude it is the Kramer Drain.

There are a few log jams in this section, but only the next one will give you trouble, and only if the water is low. The Friends have dutifully cut out the higher of several large branches, but were unable to reach the underwater branches at the time they passed through. Now they stand a few inches above the water line, and it is not possible to get your kayak across without getting out. Be careful – you will have to clamber over the wet branches while standing in swift current halfway up your thighs.

CUTLER ROAD TIMBER BRIDGE

While we may be getting bored, or at least accustomed, to flat concrete bridges with a concrete railing, Cutler Road bridge offers something different. All of its longitudinal supports and vertical pilings are made entirely of treated wood. While I have not been able to confirm it, by all appearances it was one of those constructed under a cost-sharing program offered by the U. S. Forest Service to local governments as a wood-using incentive. The program dates back several decades.

If the wind is right and in season, you will know you are near the take-out at Cutler Road by the barnyard smells from a nearby farm. It is the country, after all. This is another potential takeout point, and avoids what could otherwise be a rather long final segment. Use the left bank just before the bridge. It is a rather long climb back out to the road, where some wide spots of gravel enable car parking. I readily obtained permission from the owner, but clearly many users have skipped that step.

※ ON THE RIVER – TRIP NINE ※
(Cutler to Portland)

While up until now the Looking Glass had been, for the most part, easy-going, save for a few treefalls, big boulders, and the "dozen-rapids" section between Wright and Tallman Roads, it was time to pay a bit closer attention again and prepare for the final carnival ride. From Cutler Road to its source back upstream in Livingston County, the river has dropped at the rate of about 2.8 feet per mile. But in these last four miles we are about to experience, the river falls at double that rate. Combining this with some longer straight stretches, and now carrying its full volume of water from 70 miles of feeder streams, this final stretch of river is faster water, increasingly so as we near the Divine Highway bridge. While not particularly dangerous in moderate water levels, it was to be nonetheless a somewhat more exciting experience.

September 11 was another beautiful day. Bonnie and I started out on this final segment with the temperature in the upper 60's, just slightly after noon. Although now moving more swiftly, the water here was rather shallow and calm as we passed under the timber bridge at Cutler Road. There we immediately spotted a few larger fish. There were also schools of smaller ones and another large carp or sucker. The right bank rises quite high and slopes right down to the river's edge. A number of the overhanging maple branches were now tinged with red. This was indication that some of the previously dominant silver maples farther back

114

upstream were giving way to red maples and their characteristic color. After weaving ever so gently left and right, the river then makes a distinct bend to the right beneath the wide-spreading branches of a big white oak.

There are still a few big boulders here and there; we've scraped bottom on a few underwater stones and encountered a few rapids. After a short straight stretch, the river again turned left, and we heard a loud engine noise ahead. We soon discovered the cause, a large irrigation pump sucking water out of the river, with a strange sort of paddle wheel turning in the current. It probably supplied water to the nearby farm field. Just beyond the pump was a rock dam stretching fully across the river. Its purpose was obviously to hold back some water and thereby increase its depth for the submerged irrigation pipe. Of course, this also created a short, but notable rapids.

Soon we came upon two large sycamore trees leaning out across the river from the left. They introduce a narrower section of river forming a "tunnel of trees." It was very pretty. While the big rocks have generally diminished again, we still saw an occasional one near shore. Smaller ones remained very numerous in certain locations, most notably, as we've already pointed out, at the base of banks where the river makes a big bend. Apparently the stronger current on the outside of these bends washes away the soil, and then the numerous embedded rocks simply fall and accumulate on the river's edge.

We continued to encounter an occasional rock dam and rapids. At one point the bank on the left was again rather high, and we followed the river's bend to the right. But for the first time, this bank was sharply undercut just above the water line for some distance. There would be a couple more such banks as the day progressed. My guess is that this represents a soil layer of clay or other more structurally sound binding material, lying just above a more readily erodible kind of soil. Since the underlayer is easily washed away, the upper layer remains intact forming this interesting "bench."

The rapids are increasing again, and occasionally it was necessary to disembark and pull the kayaks across the shallower places. This was the worst section yet for that problem. Bigger rocks were also on the increase. The current continued faster and stronger, and getting hung up on a rock sideways in the current could rather easily tip and fill a kayak. Once through these rapids, we were treated to a very long view straight down the river. At its very end was a grassy opening on the left, Community Lake Park. Kayakers can readily put-in or take-out on its banks. We stopped here for a food and restroom break.

*****

The city of Portland boasts numerous parklands along both the Grand and Looking Glass Rivers. This would be the first of those to be encountered along the Looking Glass, and it is about one mile upstream from its confluence with the Grand. It is accessed by road from Rowe Avenue. Sandwiched between the river and the city's Rivertrail Linear Park, the mowed portion of this narrow park is about one third of a mile long. It also has available two pavilions, picnic facilities, modern restroom and play equipment. A small man-made pond is surrounded by cattails and fed by a bubbling spring on one end. It also provides access to the Rivertrail which completely encircles the city as a paved bike and pedestrian pathway. Long sections parallel both rivers, in this portion constructed atop the bed of an abandoned railroad route. While we ate, a car drove up, unloaded a bike, and a young man headed up the Rivertrail. Another biker passed by shortly afterward.

We then re-entered the river for the final exciting segment. An exceedingly high bank rises up on the right, with another undercut bank. Now the river becomes much narrower and deeper, at times more than waist deep, and several large fish, including bass, find it to their liking. The river itself is making a sweeping turn away from, and then back toward, the Rivertrail. This is followed by another long straight stretch,

▶ **Here we must again leave our river description for a moment to comment further on this unusual straight stretch of river. In its original and natural course, the river did not actually flow here; rather, it made a short loop a little farther to the south, on our left. In about 1869, you see, Portland got a railroad -the Ionia and Lansing Railroad. On its approach to the city from the west, it came down the long hill toward Bogue Flats, then crossed the Grand at the site of the present pedestrian/bicycle bridge just downstream of the city. There being limited land space in the valley of the Looking Glass, and facing several sweeping bends in the river, the railroad was compelled to make three bridge crossings of the Looking Glass within just a half mile. The first crossed the Looking Glass just upstream of Divine Highway and was the longest, due to the backwaters of the mill dam. The next two bridges were in quick succession due to this wide-sweeping loop to the south.**

Sometime between then and 1890, the two original railroad bridges at this site were for some reason in need of major repair or replacement. The railroad company decided it would be less cost and effort in the long run to re-route the river than to replace the two bridges. And this they did! A new channel was dug so as to remain fully north of the railroad, and eliminate the bridges. The remnants of the prior river course are evident in the stagnant oxbow, or bayou, visible at some points south of the railroad bed. Before the current fire station was built, the water-filled depression was a favored swimming hole for the boys of Portland. The railroad itself was abandoned for lack of sufficient traffic sometime between 1972 and 1986, and its old railroad bed has been converted to the pedestrian/bicycle Rivertrail. ◄

Approaching the end of this re-located river channel, we could actually hear the sound of more rapids approaching. And here again, the drop in elevation was significant and visible by simple observation. Just beyond that point three short city streets approach the Rivertrail from the south with parking at their ends. Only the first gives good access to the river, with potential for put-in, take-out and picnicking. It is Grant Street, also hosting the city's Board of Light and Power. The fire and police departments are nearby. From the river, the spot is easily identifiable by the tall observation deck/gazebo on the river's left bank, along with a huge pile of head-sized rocks piled on the bank. And, a small rapids just before the gazebo.

Leaving the gazebo behind, the river makes yet one more lazy sweep to the right. In the process, several more significant rapids must be passed, again with their accompanying drop in elevation readily visible and the water continuing faster and deeper. There is then a sharp turn to the left at the point of a high and heavily eroded bank. This is immediately followed by another notable rapids, probably the largest, longest and fastest of all on the Looking Glass, and with the most significant drop in elevation.

The river then makes its final run in a relatively straight shot for the Grand. It passes beneath the Rivertrail bridge of black metal trusses around six to eight feet tall. Originally the "Burroughs Bridge" over the Flat River, it was moved and reconstructed here. Next in sight is the traditional concrete structure of Divine Highway. This is a tricky place. A couple more rapids lie just before the bridge. Just beyond the bridge are some remains of an old dam which constrict the river, speeding it up and creating another small drop. A little more fancy paddling, and immediately beyond that is the "Canoe Landing," the final take-out, on the right.

*****

The left bank from the bridge almost to the Grand consists of a concrete retaining wall, being both a remnant of the old mill race and an effort to hinder erosion on this vulnerable steep bank at the edge of the river. It is deteriorating rather rapidly and will likely require some substantial stabilization or replacement in the coming years.

If for any reason you missed the Landing, never fear; you can probably turn around and paddle back upstream. Or, if you prefer, take out a little farther down, either on the Looking Glass or out on the Grand. Both are part of Two Rivers Park along the right shore. This area is mostly open grassland, with a band shell, parking, and several memorials to soldiers.

If you were continuing on, either intentionally or unintentionally to the Grand, you would first pass under a long foot bridge over the Looking Glass. A foot bridge had also been located here in Portland's early days. It was referred to as a "swing bridge," in my opinion because it appears to have been supported by merely a couple long cables from either shore. Cross pieces of small timbers were fastened across the cables at short intervals, and two wide planks were laid upon them for walking. It would apparently "swing" from side-to-side as a pedestrian crossed it.

The new bridge of today, constructed as part of the Rivertrail, leads up to the main through-street, Grand River Avenue, with Fabiano's River House Bar and Grill situated in the southeast corner of the intersection of the rivers. Several ice cream shops and restaurants are within walking distance. The modern city of Portland, with nearly 4,000 residents, rests upon the nearby hills.

I will shortly be telling you more about the "old dam" and the millpond which existed here. But first I want to share the account of one more historic river journey. As I've suggested several times, rivers can be dangerous, even in one so seemingly small as the Looking Glass. Listen to the telling of the story by Mrs. Betsy Webber (nee Munroe), of this near calamity which occurred right here about 180 years ago.

▶ *In the year 1837 or 1838, as there were no roads scarcely, or bridges over the rivers, they had to devise some other way for transporting goods from one place to another. In one instance a large canoe was made for this purpose, at Waterloo, or*

Wacousta, which name it now bears. This memorable boat was forty feet long, and four feet wide; and it was a gala day when this boat was launched and loaded with merchandise, to make its first trip down the Lookingglass River, into the Grand, as the terminus of the route would be Ionia, the goods belonging to Parks and Warner of that place. But as the water was high and rapid, it took six men to pole the boat ... they started down the river very nicely until they came to the milldam at Portland; the boat was unloaded, the goods carried around by hand, and the boat put over the dam and then reloaded ... the hands had some fears about passing through the mouth of the Lookingglass River, the water being very high at this season of the year. Their fears were soon realized, when the canoe swung against a large stone or rock, was split to pieces, and all was dumped in the river, the men struggling for the shore ... and the goods floating or sinking in the river, and many were entirely lost. The men were all gotten safely to shore, but very wet and cold ... The next day they returned home, on foot and by land, less courageous and wiser then when they left. ◀

❋ THE PORTLAND VICINITY ❋

▶ All of the river-mouth area was far different a couple of centuries ago. Prior to the white man's invasion of the area, an Indian campsite occupied the area near present Two Rivers Park, in the "point" of land at the mouth of the Looking Glass. It was used frequently by a small tribe under the leadership of Chief Squagen, whose principal village was just upstream at the aforementioned Shimnecon. There was also a Native cemetery at this same "point." Tradition seems to hold that both were on the north bank, but there are reasonable arguments to be made for either the north or south bank. Either might reasonably be referenced as the "point" in early accounts. But there is yet another plausible possibility, and that is that the camp was on one side, and the cemetery on the other. It was common that the place for the dead was separated from that for the living, thus making a campsite on the south bank and a cemetery on the north bank a reasonable separation. The issue, however, may never be satisfactorily resolved. There also remains the question of the eventual fate of that cemetery. There appears to be no record or recollection of whether it was eventually moved, abandoned or destroyed by future developments.

*****

Government surveys of the present Portland Township had been completed by deputy U. S. Surveyor Lucius Lyon in 1830-31, enabling land-seekers to begin claiming home and business sites. The first pioneer to purchase newly-surveyed land in Portland Township was Elisha Newman. Along with his father-in-law and younger son, James, they had come to Ann Arbor in Michigan Territory on a scouting trip. Hearing there the report of one of the original surveyors of the township that there was farther west a site with great promise as a future village, the party immediately hired ponies, along with someone familiar with the route, to guide them to the mouth of the Looking Glass.

Being very favorably impressed with the site's potential, Elisha hurried off to record his claim for a purchase of 320 acres (some sources 240 acres) including both sides of the river at its mouth. It was June of 1833. What did it take to purchase selected acreage in those days? At the time, White Pigeon, located nearly to the Indiana border, was the only Land Office in the entire area. Today, we could hop in our car at Portland and be there in less than two hours. However, Mrs. N. B. Rice, granddaughter of Mr. Newman, records a more difficult journey:

> *Finding the place met their expectations, the party went to Portage Lake, twelve miles north of Jackson, where he hired an Indian to pilot* (him) *to Jackson. From there he went to White Pigeon by stage, located* (recorded) *his land, and returned to Ann Arbor where his friends awaited.*

He would not return to the Looking Glass to take up residence until 1836.

The settlers themselves, at least here on the east side of Ionia County, had come primarily from the east, via Detroit. The tales told by these first settlers in the township mimicked those of others achieving DeWitt, and in fact, many followed those very same paths, then traveling even farther to reach the river mouth at Portland. An 1840 traveler to Ionia related that it took his family nine days by wagon from Detroit. Still another was compelled by the awful swamps to take apart his wagon and carry it piecemeal to dry land. Along the way, cooking was done by campfire along the trail, and bedding down was in tents or their wagons each night. Others spoke of fighting mosquitos and rattlesnakes, and hunting their strayed cattle. One was treed by wolves overnight while attempting to reach another settler's house.

During Elisha Newman's absence of about three years, other pioneers had arrived at the Portland site. Philo Bogue bought land in the big bend of the Grand, just a short distance downstream from the Looking Glass. Here he set up a tent and immediately established a trading post. Shortly afterward he constructed a log building, and traded not only with the Indians, but also served as storekeeper for the earliest settlers. He died in 1839, but the site still bears his name (Portland's Bogue Flats Recreation Area).

The first to build a house in Portland Township was Joshua Milne in 1833, a couple miles downstream from the present townsite. Others soon followed. Now, with numerous settlers taking up residence, supplying them with essential goods was becoming a challenge. Initially, supplies had to come either by wagon from Detroit or by water from Grand Haven, either route being difficult and expensive. In an effort to avoid the difficult tasks of transporting provisions and household goods by wagon along the poor trails aforementioned, some settlers chose to follow the route of the early French traders, and have their heaviest items transported by ship around Mackinac, thence down to Grand Haven, and then poled up the Grand River, as the Newman party would do on their return trip. This is also the early route by which some of them obtained essential supplies.

Sometime during the later 1830s, such a trip was undertaken by Almeron Newman and Lyman Bennett to obtain some items which were becoming critical locally. This required great labor, especially as one would imagine, the return trip upstream. Mr. Newman recalled:

> *I poled and Bennett pulled – that is, he walked in the river or on the shore ahead of the boat. By the time we reached Ionia we were both utterly exhausted, and, leaving our craft there, we put off overland for Portland, whence we dispatched new recruits to bring the vessel up.*

In other cases, pioneer provisions came to DeWitt, and were then poled down the Looking Glass. We've already discussed the travail associated with either of these river ventures.

Astutely aware of the situation and of course the business opportunity, Elisha returned to his property with his extended families in the spring of 1836. At the particular time of their return, the Natives had moved and set up a camp just slightly down the river on the opposite side, at Bogue Flats. The few wigwams that they had left unoccupied for a time at the Looking Glass, made of logs covered with a bark roof, served to keep the White families reasonably comfortable as they built their own cabins.

That done, Elisha and his family were ready to begin construction of a dam to power several mills. If newly-arriving residents of the new settlement and surrounding farms were able to provide for their own needs locally, they could avoid the uncertainty, expense, and time required to be supplied from other distant points. While a number of sites on both the Grand and the Looking Glass were deemed desirable as mill sites, Elisha had carefully selected the best. In 1836, a rather substantial dam, both in width and height, was built across the Looking Glass at about the location of the present day Divine Highway bridge and the Canoe Landing. By December, a sawmill had been completed near the south edge of the dam, with its long mill race running along the southern edge of the river. In January of 1837 a grinding stone was added with a bolt to mill flour. Under the direction of millwright Peter Kent, a real and proper gristmill was built for the family in 1842. These mills fell under the management of James Newman, Elisha's son. They were situated where the elongated private parking area exists today just southwest of the intersection of Divine Highway and the Looking Glass River, and stretching over toward the office of David A. Lange, C.P.A.

James's brother Almeron, following his prior trade in New York State as a clothier, pursued another business across the river, building a carding-machine in about 1850. It was the first such operation west of Pontiac. Power for this "Portland Woolen Mill" was provided by a separate race, or channel, dug between the dam and the Grand River, and located just slightly north of the main river channel. Its location would be within the open grassy field making up today's Two Rivers Park. Their families also grazed cattle and hogs, perhaps on this site, and their father Elisha fenced off the Indian cemetery to protect the gravesites, an action much appreciated by the Natives.

The village of Portland was platted around 1846. However, the naming had not been easily agreed upon. Having been called together soon after their arrival, the settlers had held a meeting for that express purpose. Such was a practical matter as mail could not readily be received without an address recognizable by the Post Office Department. Names were handed in at the meeting for consideration, but were many and varied. In the following moments of uncertainty, Abram Hixson offered the name "Portland," which seemed fitting as there was "a fine landing, where all the passing boats stopped." This met the pleasure of the group and was adopted. It was recognized as an official post office in 1837. Mail was now received once a week by carriers on horseback until about 1846, when they were replaced by stage coaches. To receive their mail, recipients had to offer up 25 cents, a sum which was not always readily available. Mockingly, a writer sending one such letter from Vermont to Mr. Bazateel Taft in Kalamazoo, Michigan at the time was addressed:

For Kalamo I'm bound, Uncle Sam,
To Bazateel Taft in Michigan;
When you get there you'll see his log fence,
Then ask him for the twenty-five cents.

*****

While a village and mills were favored by Portland's location on two rivers, it did provide a logistical problem for the frequent need to pass from one side to the other. Originally the residents, and presumably the earliest pioneers on the Grand River Trail, used the shallow ford on the Grand, at the spot of the lower bridge, that being Grand River Avenue. A flat-boat ferry was also used, but might often require several trips to bring across all of one's belongings. Smaller canoes were also in common use for transport of lighter items. A simple foot-bridge was later added at this point, said to be built on "benches" covered with planks. Obviously when the river rose in springtime or after a hard rain, there was a scramble to remove the planks to avoid their being swept away. Sometimes in winter the ice on either river would be thick enough to support a wary traveler. A few years later, in 1837 or 38, a bridge was finally built upstream (today's Bridge Street), and eventually another at the location of the old ford (today's Grand River Avenue).

Should anyone in the town, or anywhere else within 40 miles take sick or have an accident, only a few physicians were available to respond. In 1833 Dr. W. B. Lincoln settled in Ionia, and was often called upon to ride horseback everywhere from Grand Rapids to the DeWitt settlement, and just as far to the north and south. His big leather saddlebags would be stuffed with a variety of remedies and instruments, and he readily attended to both White and Native in need. Several pioneers, however, completely lacking in access to any medical aid on their journey, had buried family members along the Looking Glass trail. ◄

Yes, a few had died along the trail, still others while making their homes in the wilderness, and some just as the result of daily struggles against hardship, wild beasts, injuries and disease. But both these, and those who survived were a brave and hardy lot, pursuing opportunities in a new land. Fortunately, their stories and memories linger for us to ponder and appreciate.

❋ REFLECTING ❋

Like these earliest pioneers, though in a different sense, our journey down the historic Looking Glass was also complete. Much of it was as anticipated: an easy-going river, scenic vistas, tree-lined banks. But there were also some surprises: lots of huge boulders, numerous rapids, mostly undeveloped frontage, an eagle and a multitude of other wildlife, and a rich history.

Much of it would appear today the same as it had to those earliest pioneers. Some of it would not. Bridges are now constructed at nearly every mile. Beautiful homes, and entire subdivisions, can be glimpsed in some areas. Nostalgia for the look of the "old days" is a strong force in me, so I had some personal regrets over these and other signs of "progress."

▶ I doubt, however, that the early settlers would agree. Listen to some of their later-life reflections as they looked back over their lifetimes and recorded their own feelings. Here are just a few examples:

N. Covey, 1834, on the departure of her brother John Nowlin and his family from their native New York, to a place "out of the world" (Michigan):
> *Dear Brother and Sister, we must bid you adieu,*
> *We hope that the Lord will deal kindly with you,*
> *Protect and defend you, wherever you go,*
> *If Christ is your friend, sure you need fear no foe.*
>
> *The distance doth seem great, to which you are bound,*
> *But soon we must travel on far distant ground,*
> *And if we prove faithful to God's grace and love,*
> *If we ne'er meet before, we shall all meet above.*

John Nowlin, 1875: Some years after our landing at Detroit, I saw the steamboat "Michigan" and thought of the perilous time we had on her coming up Lake Erie (in 1834). *She was then an old boat, and was laid up. I thought of the many thousand hardy pioneers she had brought across the turbulent lake and landed safely on the shore of the territory whose name she bore.*

(**My father**) *did not often refer to the hardships which he had endured in Michigan; but often spoke of the privations and endurance of others. Thus, in his latter days, not thinking of what he had done, he seemed to feast on the idea, that America had produced such and such ones, who had been benefactors and effectual workers for the good of our race.*

Most of those men who came here in the prime of life, about the time that father came, are gone. The country shows what they have done, but few consider it properly. Some know what it was then and what it is now and know also, that it has arrived at the exalted position it now occupies through the iron will, clear brain and the steady unflinching nerve of others. Yet they pass on in their giddy whirl and the constant excitement of the nineteenth century, when wealth is piled at their doors, and hardly think of their silent benefactors.

When I was quite young ... Mr. Elijah Lord came and settled about a mile and a half north-west of father's. He came down with his oxen by father's place to get small, hard-maple trees, out of the woods, that he wanted to take home and set out on his place ... He set out the trees on both sides of the road ... I asked him if he expected to see them grow up; he said he did not set them out for himself, but for the benefit of other people, for the good of the generations that would follow him.

Milo M. Quaife, 1937, reflecting on the long-past times of John Nowlin, (above): The hand of the subdivider is upon all the region; the pioneer homes ... have vanished, along with the red man, the timber, and the black ash swamps ... His living descendants are scattered far and wide; the ancestral acres have passed into the hands of strangers, busy in their turn with the labors and problems which everyday living presents.

Mrs. Cornelia Daniells Hazard, 1904, reflecting on her family's early days (1849+) in Wacousta: ... leaving the comforts of a higher civilization and coming into this then dense wilderness to carve out a home for themselves ... that their children and their children's children might reap the fruits of their noble and heroic sacrifices ... none took their lot as a hard one, or dreamt they were heroes or heroines – all went to their daily duties with a cheerfulness and bravery that would put to shame many a one far better situated in those days.

When I enter upon this subject I do not know where to leave of (**off the**) *details and incidents which, through the many intervening years, may have become dimmed to me, but the general impression seems almost as vivid to me as though memories of a few years. But now nearly all are gone, only a few are left to look back upon those scenes, which to this generation no picture can paint and no pen fully describe.* ◄

*****

As today's citizens contemplate the trials faced by the earliest settlers - fearful of prowling wolves, bears, and cougars; establishing homesteads in a wilderness; and facing huge difficulties just to survive, I doubt many of us would criticize too harshly their welcoming of the overall change. We will simply be thankful that we today can in fact still enjoy the best of both the PAST and the PRESENT Looking Glass River.

1. The source of the Looking Glass River.
North side of Sober Road, Livingston County.
Photo by author.

2. One of many miles of county drains. Upper Looking Glass, looking east from Stow Road. Photo by author.

3. 1875 map of Glass River (ghost town), showing buildings, mills, dam and mill pond.
Photo courtesy of HistoricMapWorks.com

4. One of many marshlands bordering the upper river.
Photo by author.

5. Babcock Landing, now a MDNR Public Access Site. Photo by author.

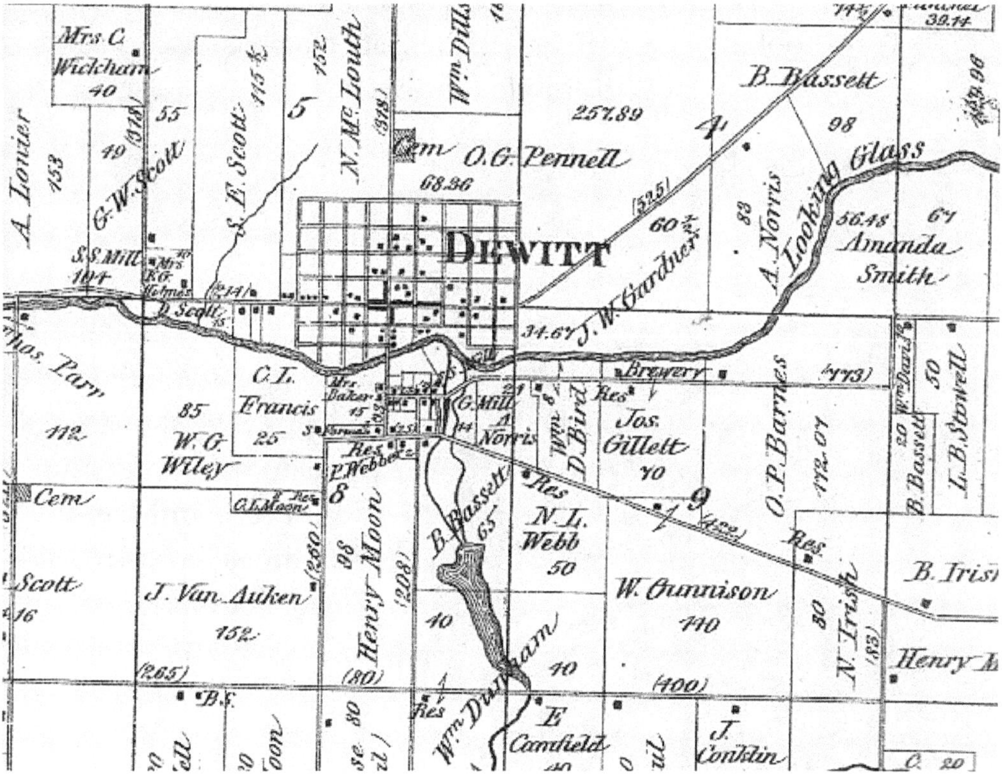

6. 1873 map showing Prairie Creek, dam and backwaters and water courses. Photo from 1873 Clinton County plat map.

7. Interurban on the DeWitt trestle over the Looking Glass River. 1917. Photo courtesy of DeWitt Public Library, P81.

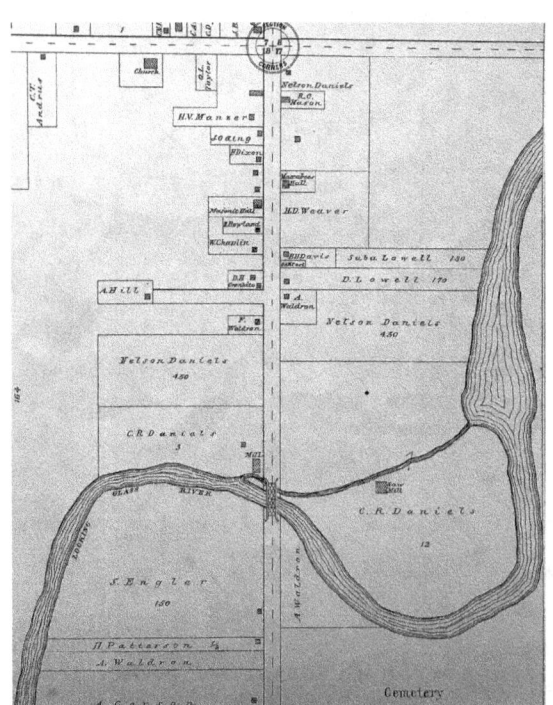

8. Map of Wacousta area, 1896, showing dam backwaters, mill race, mills and buildings. From 1896 map of unknown source.

9. Author's son, Todd, passes by one of many huge boulders in the river. Photo by author.

10. The McCrumb sawmill near Grange Road, 1881. Note the mill race as it re-joins the river. Photo courtesy of the Jeanne Bewersdorff collection.

11. Dam near the mouth of the river at Portland, 1908. Shadowy building on the right is the mill. Photo courtesy of Robert Torp-Smith

12. Mouth of the Looking Glass River today, as it joins the Grand River at Portland. Photo by author.

BIBLIOGRAPHY

Arbanas, Larry. Personal communications., November 10, 2017, and afterward.
Babcock, William Jr. Personal communications, May 20, 2017.
Babcock, William Sr. and Estelle. Personal communications, March 4, 2017, and afterward.
"Baptist Brethren Record Book." DeWitt, Michigan, 1840-1856.
Barnett, LeRoy. "Kindness and Comestibles on the Michigan Frontier." *Chronicle*, Volume 39, No. 2., Summer, 2016.
Barnett, LeRoy, Ph.D. "The First Published Map of Wacousta." 1873.
Beers, F.W., Supt. *Atlas of Livingston County, Michigan.* New York: F.W. Beers & Co., 1875.
BeGole, Brian. Personal communications, December 28, 2016, and afterward.
Bergan, Kristin. "History of Wacousta." Personal essay.
Bewersdorff, Jeanne. Personal communications, May 17, 2017, and afterward.
"Biological and Water Chemistry Surveys of Selected Stations in the Looking Glass River Watershed." Michigan Department of Environmental Quality, Water Bureau, July, 2008.
Bishop, Bob. Personal communications, 2013.
"Black Ash Basketry: A Story of Cultural Resilience." A documentary DVD by the Great Lakes Lifeways Institute, 2010.
"Black bear population booming in northern Michigan." Briefs in the *Lansing State Journal*, February 16, 2017. (Vol. 162, No. 288).
Blois, John T. *Gazetteer of the State of Michigan*. Detroit: Sydney L. Rood & Co., 1840.
Branch, E.E., editor. *History of Ionia County, Michigan, Vol. I.* Indianapolis, Indiana: B.F. Bowen and Company, Inc.,1916.
"Building – Structure Inventory Form." Nomination forms for the State Register of Historic Sites. Michigan History Division, Michigan Department of State, 1990.
"Business Plan for NHD Implementation." Michigan Association of County Drain Commissioners (MACDC), 2014.
"Carte Des Lacs Du Canada." 1744. Michigan State University library.
Castro, Joseph. "Who Invented the Mirror?" Live Science, Everett Collection.
www.livescience.com/34466-who-invented-mirror.html

(accessed December 20, 2016).

Ceasar, Ford Stevens. "Forgotten Communities of Central Michigan." An address given to meeting of the Greater Lansing Historical Society, May, 1963.

"Clinton County Places." Genealogists of the Clinton County Historical Society. www.dewittlibrary.org/cchs/places.pdf (accessed March 2, 2017).

Coin, Kenneth. *DeWitt Area History*. DeWitt Public Library, DeWitt, Michigan, 1983 and 2008.

County Atlas of Shiawassee County, Michigan, 1875. F.W. Beers and Co., 1875.

Daboll, Judge S.B. *Past and Present of Clinton County, Michigan*. Chicago: The S.J. Clarke Publishing Company, 1906.

"Deed of Chandler Marsh." Clinton County Arhives.

"DeWitt Community History." City of DeWitt. www.dewittmi.org/OurCommunity/CommunityHistory/FullHistory.aspx (accessed December 17, 2016).

"DeWitt, Michigan." http://en.wikipedia.org/wiki/DeWitt,_Michigan (accessed December 12, 2016)

Dunham, Irene (Babcock). Personal communications, May 20, 2017.

"Echoes of Yesteryears, Shiawassee County Schools, Antrim and Perry Townships, Volume B, 1837-1987."

Evers, David C., editor. *Endangered and Threatened Wildlife of Michigan*. Ann Arbor: The University of Michigan Press, 1994.

"Frequently Asked Questions." Bay County info re: Drains, 2017. Website: drainoffice@baycounty.net (accessed January 14, 2017).

Fletcher, Doc. *Michigan Rivers Less Paddled*. Traverse City, Michigan: Arbutus Press, 2009.

Friends of the Looking Glass. "Looking Glass RiverTrail Guide." Clinton Conservation District, St. Johns, Michigan, 2009.

Friends of the Looking Glass. "Looking Glass River Watershed Handbook." 1999.

Friends of the Looking Glass. "The Looking Glass River – The History of a Township and Regional Treasure." *DeWitt Township Newsletter*, November, 2012, and March, 2013.

Galardi, Rick. "How Are Things in the Township?" *DeWitt Charter Township Newsletter*, Summer, 2007.

"Glass River Cemetery, Shiawassee County." With some information collected by Diana Dempsey, 2001. http://www.mi-roots.org (accessed December 26, 2016).

"Glass River Odd Fellows Town Hall." A postcard-like image in the

Shiawassee County Historical Museum. Copied January 19, 2017.

"Glass River." With some information submitted by Mike Steele. www.ghosttowns.com/bottom.html (accessed December 26, 2016).

Godfrey, Linda S. *Weird Michigan.* New York, NY: Sterling Publishing Co., Inc., 2006.

Greco, Rachel. "The oldest surviving student recalls 'how awful it was.'" *DeWitt-Bath Review,* May 14, 2017. (Vol. 45, No. 29)

Gurski, Brad, Director of Operations, Southern Clinton County Municipal Utilities Authority. Personal communications, March, 2017.

Hagel, Jeremy. "Eagle's last old bridge falls." *Clinton County News,* December 30, 2001. (Vol. 145, No. 39).

Hazard, Mrs. Cornelia. "The First School – Reminiscence of Early Pioneer Days." Presentation given on November 24, 1904, at Watertown Center School House.

Hazard, Mrs. Cornelia. "The Early History of Wacousta." Memoir written in 1918.

Hinsdale, Wilbert B. *Archaeological Atlas of Michigan.* Michigan Handbook Series, No. 4. Ann Arbor: The University of Michigan Press, 1931.

History and Directory of Ionia County, Michigan. Grand Rapids, Michigan: J.D. Dillenback, 1872.

The History of Clinton County, Michigan. The Clinton County Historical Society, St. Johns, Michigan, 1980.

"History of Laingsburg." Laingsburg Business and Community Association, 2017.

History of Shiawassee County and Its Townships. www.migenweb.org/shiawassee/history.html (accessed January 4, 2017).

History of Shiawassee and Clinton Counties, Michigan. Philadelphia: D.W. Ensign & Co., 1880.

"History of Storm Drainage." Cass County Michigan Governmental Offices, 2016. www.casscountymi.org/Home/DrainCommission/HistoryofStormDrainage.aspx (accessed January 5, 2017).

"History of the Tri-County Region." Information Report 7. Tri-County Regional Planning Commission, Lansing, August, 1984.

"A History of the Village of Morrice." www.morrice.mi.us (accessed December 16, 2016).

Hollister, O.C. "Wacousta." *The Clinton Republican*, March 26, 1914.

"How Indians Built Canoes." International Film Bureau Presentation, 1946. A video by Masters of Survival. youtube.com/watch?v=enMSwz5BWGo

"Indian Trails." www.geo.msu.edu/geogmich/indian_trails.html (accessed December, 2016).

"Ionia and Lansing Railroad." http://en.wikipedia.org/wiki/ionia_and_Lansing_Railroad. (accessed November 4, 2017).

Irland, Lloyd, and McWilliams, Will. "The Lake States Tamarack Resource: An Opportunity for Small Landowners?" *National Woodlands,* Autumn, 2016. (Vol. 39, No. 4).

Lake, D.J. *Atlas of Clinton County, Michigan.* Philadelphia: C.O. Titus, 1873.

Lash, Darren. Personal communications, June 30, 2017, and afterward.

Lavey, Kathleen. "DNR confirms sighting of cougar in Bath Township." *Lansing State Journal*, June 30, 2017. (Vol. 163, No. 57).

"A Leading Historic Bridge Resource." Website. HistoricBridges.org (accessed February 23, 2017).

Longyear, Harriet Munro. "The Settlement of Clinton County, Michigan." Michigan Historical Collections, Volume XXXIX, 1915.

"Looking Glass River." http://en.wikipedia.org/w/index.php?title=Looking_Glass_River&oldid=756771486 (accessed January 12, 2017).

"Looking Glass River Watershed Management Plan." GLRC on Phase II. March 31, 2006.

Map of the Counties of Clinton and Gratiot, Michigan. Philadelphia: Samuel Geil Publisher, 1864.

Martin, Jean. "Wacousta was formerly known as Waterloo." *Clinton County News*, November 15, 1978.

"Memorial Addresses on the Life and Character of Zachariah Chandler." Delivered in the Senate and House of Representatives, January 28, 1880. Washington: Government Printing Office, 1880.

"Michigan Department of Transportation Drainage Manuel." Michigan Department of Transportation and Tetra Tech MPS, January, 2006.

"Michigan's Historic Bridges." Michigan Department of Transportation (website) (accessed February 23, 2017).

Michigan Nature Association (website) www.michigannature.org (accessed February 15, 2017).

Michigan Pioneer and Historical Collections. Volume II. Detroit: Wm. Graham's Presses, 52 Bates Street, 1880.

Michigan Pioneer and Historical Collections. Volume V. Lansing, Michigan: W.S. George & Co., State Printers and Binders, 1884.

Michigan Pioneer and Historical Collections. Volumes XIV (1908), XVII (1910), XVIII (1911), XXI (1912-13) and XXX (1906). Lansing, Michigan: Wynkoop Hallenbeck Crawford Company, State Printers.

Michigan Pioneer and Historical Collections. Volume XXVI. Lansing: Robert Smith & Co., State Printers and Binders, 1896.

Michigan Wildlife Conservancy (letter). "Comments on Proposed Rule to Remove the Eastern Cougar from the Federal List of Endangered and Threatened Species." August 10, 2015.

Michigan Wildlife Conservancy. "Living with Cougars in Michigan." www.miwildlife.org/cougars.html (accessed December 15, 2016).

Miller, Gloria, founder and past president, Friends of the Looking Glass River Watershed Council. Personal communications, July 7, 2017, and afterward.

Miller, Gloria. "Memories" of My Looking Glass. Unpublished essay.

Morrison, Jon. Engineer/Deputy Drain Commissioner, Clinton County Drain Commission. Personal communications, July 10, 2017, and afterward.

Mulford, Charlotte A. "Schavey Road Family Farm has a Long History.*" DeWitt-Bath Review*, August 6, 2017. (Vol. 45, No. 41).

"Native Americans in the Great Lakes Region." Michigan State University. www.geo.msu.edu/extra/geogmich/paleo-indian.html (accessed December, 2016).

Nickel, Walt. "Kraft's is Oldest Wacousta Store." Newspaper clipping of unknown origin.

"Nonagenarian Recalls Childhood Days, Indians, in Victor Township." *The Laingsburg Press*, March 9, 1950.

Nowlin, John. *The Bark Covered House*. Detroit: Printed for the author, 1876.

Ogle, George A. *Standard Atlas of Clinton County, Michigan*. Chicago: Geo. A. Ogle & Co., 1896.

Ogle, George A. *Standard Atlas of Clinton County, Michigan*. Chicago: Geo. A. Ogle & Co., 1915.

Opolka, Frank, and Leone, John. "Public Rights on Michigan Waters." Law Enforcement Division (MDNR), March 22, 2010.

The Past and Present, Shiawassee County, Michigan, Historically. The Michigan Historical Publishing Association, 1906.

Peters, Julie (Staines). "Earlier Wacousta." May, 2006.

Pitawanakwat, Alphonse. Nokomis Learning Center, Okemos, Michigan.

Personal communications, February 20, 2017, and afterward.
Pulver, Joseph, Managing Director, Clinton County Road Commission. Personal communications, March, 2017.
Reed Cemetery Headstones, Laingsburg. Grave Search Results. www.findagrave.com/cgi-bin/fg.cgi?page=cr&CRid=1453 (accessed March 5, 2017).
Reuschel, Theodore, and Reuschel, Bonita. *The Story of Aral, Benzie County, Michigan*. Michigan History Division, Department of State, 1978.
"Report: Cougars killed in Michigan likely born elsewhere." *Lansing State Journal*, October 20, 2016. (Vol. 162, No. 169).
Rice, Mrs. N. B. "Early History of Portland, Michigan." ImagesofMichigan.com. (accessed November 4, 2017).
Romig, Walter. *Michigan Place Names*. Detroit: Wayne State University Press, 1986.
Rusz, Patrick J. Personal communications, 2016.
Rusz, Patrick J. "The Cougar in Michigan: Sightings and Related Information." Technical publication of the Bengel Wildlife Center. February, 2001.
"Safety Inspection Report of Lake Geneva Dam ID # 617." Wilcox Professional Services, LLC, May, 2012.
Schenck, John S. *History of Ionia and Montcalm Counties, Michigan*. Philadelphia: D.W. Ensign and Co., 1881.
Scott, Gene. "Michigan Shadow Towns." September, 2005.
"Shimnecon cemetery." www.findagrave.com/cgi-bin/fg.cgi?page=cr&CRid=2304464 (accessed February 14, 2017).
Shumaker, Sharon. Personal communications, May 20, 2017.
"So Where Does All That Water Go, Anyway?" *DeWitt Township Newsletter*, March, 2013.
Southern Clinton County Municipal Utilities Authority. Website. www.sccmua.com/Default.aspx?tabid=2072 (accessed January 31, 2017).
"Stormwater Management: It all ends up in the Grand River." 2014. www.dewitttownship.org/Our Environment/StormwaterManagement.aspx.
Summers, Wayne. Personal communications, July 18, 2017, and afterward.
"Take a Kid Fishing! Mid-Michigan: Guide to Public Lakes and Rivers."
Townsend, T.H. "Watertown History." *The Clinton Republican*, September 7, 1905.
"Victor Pioneer." Obituary of Duane Babcock. *The Clinton Republican*, January 28, 1906.

"Wacousta, Michigan." www.wacousta.org/about.htm (accessed February 10, 2017).

Wacousta, typed notes, source unknown. Grand Ledge Area District Library at Wacousta.

Wanless, Lt. Thomas. (MDNR) Personal communications. June 5, 2017.

Ward, Mark. Personal communications. June 22, 2017, and afterward.

"Wigwam." https://en.wikipedia.org/w/index.php?title=wigwam&oldid=762218105 (accessed February 2, 2017).

Wright, Linda. Personal communications, May 1, 2017.

Ziibiwing Center. (brochures and exhibits) The Saginaw Chippewa Indian Tribe of Michigan. Mt. Pleasant, Michigan, March, 2017.

General Index

Adams, David D. 19, 23
Adams, John C. 19, 22
Airport road 30, 53, 73, 75, 82-83
Antrim 20, 22
Antrim Center 24
Arbanas, Larry 14, 26, 75

Babcock family 38-41
Babcock's Landing/Lake/road 29, 34, 36, 38-43
Basket 55
Bath road 24
Bauer road 86
Beard, Allen 18, 22-23
Beard road 16-21
Bee Hive 63
BeGole family 19
Bennett, Lyman 121-122
Bewersdorff, Jeanne 106
Blinston, Joseph 22-23
Bogue Flats 116, 121-122
Bogue, Philo 121
Boy Scouts 85
Braden road 16-17
Bridge street 59-60, 62-63, 72
Brimley road 7
Britton road 25
Buttonbush 51

Campau, George 60
Calder, James 95
Canoe, Indian 53, 55-57, 73, 99
Canoe Landing 118, 122
Cardinal Flower 82
Cass, Terr. Gov. 9
Chandler Farm 111
Chandler Marsh 49

Chandler road 40, 42-44, 47, 49-50
Chandler, Zachariah 48
Clark road 58, 98-100
Clean water facility 75-76, 82
Clinton, DeWitt 65
Clinton House 62
Clinton, James 65
Clinton, name 64, 66
Copley, Alexander B. 79
Coin, Kenneth 64, 71-72
Colby road 25
Community Lake Park 115
Cork road 18
County drains 5-6, 8, 11-12, 15, 25-26, 47-48, 74, 87, 113
Covey, N. 125
Cutler drain 88
Cutler road 40, 75, 113-114

Dam and/or mill
  Faiver drain 75
  Glass River 17-23
  McCrumb 106
  Oliver's 72
  Portland 93, 119, 122-123
  Prairie Creek 58, 61-63
  Scott's 63
  Summers drain 85
  Wacousta 62, 91-93, 105-106
Daniells, Cornelia 90, 94, 126
Daniells, Nathaniel 91
Daniels, Nelson 94
Dempsey, Diana 23
Detroit 9, 18-19, 48-49, 54, 66, 68, 79-80, 95, 102, 121, 125
DeWitt 29, 39, 43, 45-47, 50-52, 58-59, 61, 63-64, 67, 70-72, 76, 78-79, 81, 87, 89, 94, 98-99, 102, 121-122, 124
DeWitt House 63

DeWitt Millenium Garden Club 59
DeWitt, name 64, 66
DeWitt road 30, 58
Dill street 61
Divine Hwy. 114, 116-117, 122
Duckweed 36-37, 39
Dugout 56, 80-81
Dwarf Lake Iris 36

Eden trail 80, 98, 103
Ellsworth road 16, 19, 21, 24
Erie Canal 65-66, 80, 94

Fabiano's River House Bar and Grill 118
Faiver drain 75
Floodplain 25, 28-29, 38, 74
Foote, Don 71
Forest Hill road 86
Francis road 85
Friends of the Looking Glass 27, 31, 70, 75, 78-79, 83, 104, 113

Girl Scouts 93
Glass River 17, 20, 22-24
Gloria Miller Looking Glass Valley Park 89
Godfrey road 19, 21, 23-24
Grand River trail (see Indian trails)
Grange road 105-107, 109
Granger Landfill 30
Grant street 117
Grape Vine 102, 110
Greeley, Horace 9
Groger, Stephen 79-80, 98, 102, 108

Halterman, Peter 63
Harlow's Canoe Livery 97

Harlow, Betty J. 97
Harmon brothers 19
Hazard, Cornelia Daniells 94, 126
Hazelton, G.H. 45
Hemmingway Lake 7
Herbison road 58, 62, 72, 75-77, 82, 86, 88-89, 108
Heritage Park 88
Herrington road 6-7
Hinman, John 65
Hinman road 15, 96, 104-105
Hixson, Abram 123
Holiday Haven Girl Scouts 91
Howe road 47, 71, 109, 111-112
Husted-Landenburg drain 98

Indians (see Native Americans)
Indian Green 51-52, 54, 58, 60
Indian trails 18, 24, 27, 45, 53, 60, 80, 87, 89, 100
Interurban 58-59

Jegla, Dennis and Shelly 96
Jerusalem Artichoke 110
Jewelweed 110
Joe Pye Weed 104
Jones, Cammie 78
Jopi 104

Kent, Peter 122
Kramer drain 113
Krepp's road 46

La Hontan, French Baron 9
Laing, Peter 28, 40
Laingsburg 24-25, 27-28, 39, 41, 54, 76
Lake Geneva 70-72
Lake Michigan 7, 53-54, 68
Lake Huron 7, 53
Lange, David A. CPA 122

Lincoln, Dr. W.B. 124
Lizard's Tail Flower 50-51
Locust street 61
Longyear, Harriet (Munro) 10, 100
Looking Glass Garden Club 86,
Looking Glass, name 67-69
Looking Glass Riverfront Park 82
Lord, Elijah 126
Lovejoy road 16
Lowell road 84
Lowry, John 44-46
Lowry, Olivia 44
Lowry Plains 44-45
Lyon, Lucius 120

MacArthur, Gen. Duncan 9
Malaria 10-11
Maple River 12, 53, 68, 107
Maple sugar/syrup 56-57, 102
McCrumb, George W. 106
McGuire Park 52, 70
Meade, Marshall 108
Melvin, Lyman 18
Memorial Park 59
Middletown 61, 67
Mill (see dam and/or mill)
Miller, Gloria 26, 79, 85, 87, 89, 92, 96
Milne, Joshua 121
Monroe road 111, 113
Morrice 23, 30
Morrice, William 23
Mullett, John 108
Munger, Thomas 19
Munro, Harriet 10, 99-100

Native Americans 8, 10, 18, 24, 27, 30, 43-44, 51-57, 60, 68-70, 72-73, 79, 83, 87, 94-96, 102, 104, 110, 120-124
Navigation, legal 13-15
Navigation, physical 15-16
Near, John 21-22
New Albany 61-63
Newman, Almeron 121
Newman, Elisha 120-122
Newman, James 122
Niles, Anthony 79-81, 98-99, 102, 108
Niles Creek 98-99
Niles, Mrs. M.J. 10
Niles road 98-100
Niles Settlement 15, 98-100
Nohel road 5, 16
Nokomis Learning Center 69
Nowlin, John 10, 12, 65, 100, 125-126

Oak openings 18, 32, 111
Old 27- 42, 47, 50, 52, 58
Old DeWitt 61-62
Oliver, Franklin 72
Openlander drain 97

Park Lake 49
Patrick road 108
Peters, Julie (Staines) 93, 96
Pickerel Weed 46
Pitawanakwat, Alphonse 69, 95
Pontiac 54, 60, 80, 102, 122
Pontiac and Grand River trail (see Indian trails)
Portland 4, 14, 30, 53-54, 81, 93, 98, 100, 114, 116-123
Portland Woolen Mill 122
Prairie Creek 58, 61-63
Purdy, Josiah 23

Quaife, Milo 126

Rathburn, Dyer 18

Red Cedar River 6-7
Remy-Chandler Intercounty
    Drain 47-48, 50
Rice, Mrs. N.B. 100-101, 120
Riverside Park 59
RiverTrail guide 4, 14, 28, 34
Rivertrail Linear Park 116
Rowland, Henry 100
Roy, Kari 78
Rusz, Dr. Patrick J. 33

Saginaw River 7, 107
Sauger Lake 7
Scott, Capt. David 45-46, 52,
    60-63, 79-81, 89, 99, 102
Scott's 62-63
Schavey road 71-73
Schoewe, Theodore 72
Shiawassee River 7, 12, 24, 53,
    107
Shimnecon 43, 119
Silsbee, Benjamin 96
Sober road 6-7, 16
Source 4-8, 14-17, 25, 73, 114
Squagen, Chief 119
State road 5, 17, 30
Storm water 11, 74-75, 77
Stowell, Hiram 44, 46
Stow road 6, 8, 12
String Algae 110
Summers drain 85
Surveys, orig. govt. 8-9, 43, 49,
    53, 67-68, 108, 111, 120

Taft, Bazateel 123
Tallman road 104, 107, 113-114
Tiffin, Edward 9
Tiger Lilies 50
Tipi/teepee 54
Townsend, Mr. 108
Townsend, T.H. 95
Turner, Jesse and Milo 61-62

Turner road 58
Twin Lakes 7
Two Rivers Park 118-119, 123

Upper Wilds 28
US 127- 46
Upton road 4, 14, 27-28, 34,
    39-40

Wabwaysin 68
Wacousta 62, 69, 82, 88-89,
    91-92, 94-95, 97, 105-106,
    119, 126
Wacousta General Store 88-89,
    96
Wacousta road 86, 88, 91-93, 96
Wanless, Lt. Thomas R. 14-15
Ward, Mark 26
Wassololo 27
Waterloo 89, 94-95, 118
Water quality 74, 77
Watershed 3-4, 7-8, 28, 30-34,
    37, 50, 56, 76-79, 100, 112
Webb road 49
Webber, Betsy (Munroe) 30,
    118
White Water Lily 44
Wigwam 54-55, 60, 81, 122
Wilcox. Hiram 61
Wolf Creek 6-7
Wood road 30, 47
Woodbury road 14, 25
Wright, Issac 19
Wright, Linda 22
Wright road 97-98, 104, 107,
    113-114
Wright, Walter 19, 22-23

Yellow Water Lily 46-47

www.ingramcontent.com/pod-product-compliance
Lightning Source LLC
Chambersburg PA
CBHW070103080526
44586CB00013B/1173